Riding the

Roller Coaster

MARJA BERGEN

Riding the
Roller Coaster
LIVING WITH
MOOD DISORDERS

Northstone

Editors: Michael Schwartzentruber, Dianne Greenslade
Cover design: Margaret Kyle
Cover artwork: Julie Elliot
Interior design: Julie Bachewich
Consulting art director: Robert MacDonald

Northstone Publishing acknowledges the financial support of the Government of Canada through the Book Publishing Industry Development Program for its publishing activities.

Northstone Publishing is an imprint of Wood Lake Books Inc., an employee-owned company, and is committed to caring for the environment and all creation. Northstone recycles, reuses, and composts, and encourages readers to do the same. Resources are printed on recycled paper and more environmentally friendly groundwood papers (newsprint), whenever possible. The trees used are replaced through donations to the Scoutrees for Canada program. Ten percent of all profit is donated to charitable organizations.

"Patterns of Bipolar Disorder" illustration from *Bipolar Disorder: Where's the Balance?* 1995/1996, Alberta Health. Used by permission.

Canadian Cataloguing in Publication Data
Bergen, Marja, 1946–
Riding the Roller Coaster
ISBN 1–896836–31–3
1. Manic-depressive illness. 2. Mania. 3. Depression, Mental. I. Title.
RC537.B47 1999 616.89'5 C98–911205–5

Published by Northstone Publishing
an imprint of Wood Lake Books Inc.
Kelowna, British Columbia, Canada

Printing 10 9 8 7 6 5 4 3 2
Printed in Canada by Transcontinental Printing & Graphics Inc.

Contents

Acknowledgments 9

Foreword 12

Introduction 14

1. WHAT IS A MOOD DISORDER?

What is a Mood Disorder? 19

Depression 20

Mania 21

Psychosis 24

A Roller-Coaster Ride 26

Patterns of Bipolar Disorder 27

Keeping a Balance 28

An Illness Like Any Other 30

Dealing With the Stigma 31

2. GETTING HELP

Denial 37

Getting Help 37

Medications 38

Psychotherapy 40

Finding a Good Doctor 41

Hospital Revisited 42

If You Can Trust Yourself 44

3. WHEN WE ARE DEPRESSED

When We Are Depressed 47

Caught In a Dream World 48

When Life Doesn't Seem Worth Living 51

Things to Do When You Don't Feel Like Doing Anything .. 53

Things to Do When You Can Cope a Little 54

Things to Do When You Feel Stronger 54

Anxiety 55

4. WHEN WE ARE MANIC

With Feet Firmly On the Ground 59

Overstimulation 60

After Mania 63

Self-esteem 65

Attitudes to Build Self-esteem 66

5. KEEPING LIFE STABLE

Keeping Life Stable 71

Managing Stress 72

Physical Exercise 73

Relaxation 74

Relaxation Techniques 75

Nutritious Eating 77

Comfort Foods 77

Handling Our Finances 79

Quiet Times 80

Sleeplessness 82

Combating Loneliness 83

6. SUPPORTIVE RELATIONSHIPS

Supportive Relationships 87

Family 89

Friendship 91

Spiritual Support 92

Self-help Groups 93

The Telephone 94

Journaling 95

7. A SPIRITUAL SOURCE OF STRENGTH

Spirituality 99

Faith 100

Patience 104

Hope 104

Forgiving Others and Ourselves 106

Love 107

Being Grateful 109

The Positive Side of Suffering 111

Moving Beyond Ourselves 112

8. BUILDING CONFIDENCE

Building Confidence 119

The Importance of Being Active 120

Rise, Check Your Diary, and Shine! 121

Finding Meaning In Life 123

Pursuing a Goal 124

Overcoming Obstacles 125

Work is Precious 126

Building: Skills, Talents, Hobbies, Career 128

Responsibility 130

Stepping Stones of Life 133

9. THE CREATIVE RESPONSE

The Creative Response 139

Artists with Mood Disorders 141

Those Not Altogether Unlike Us 142

Our Passions, High and Low 144

Our Need to Be Unique 146

Child's Play 146

To Be a Master 148

When Our Imagination Takes Control 149

Begin It! 149

Conclusion 151

Appendix: Mood Disorder Self-help Groups,
Internet Web Sites, and Newgroups 153

The grand essentials to happiness
in this life are
something to do,
something to love,
and something to hope for.

- Joseph Addison

Acknowledgments

This book would not have been possible without the help and encouragement of many big-hearted people. There are so many friends and family members who support me in so many ways; the list I include here is by no means complete. I will only include the names of individuals who, I find, had the most direct influence on my well-being and the eventual production of this book. It is with much gratitude that I remember them.

At the top of the list of those I am indebted to is my husband and best friend, Wes. Throughout my ups and downs, those many times I was hard to live with, he remained patient and supportive. He never failed to show me his love, even when I wasn't very lovable. With his help it has been possible to live a secure and stable lifestyle.

I thank my son, Cornelius (Jeff), for giving me such joy, both when he was a little guy, and now as a grown man. Dad (now deceased) and Mom, my sisters, Ann and Ineke, as well as Wes's mom and dad and extended family (including many aunts, uncles and cousins) all surround my life with a priceless circle of love. I'm tremendously fortunate to have all these folks close by.

I often think with gratitude of Bert Cowan, the office manager who trusted me with a job when I was fresh out of Riverview Hospital. His belief in me helped me get back on my feet and learn to believe in myself again.

I'll be forever grateful for the care given me by Dr. Gerald McDougall during the initial ten years of my illness. It was so good of him to encourage me to stay in touch when he couldn't be my doctor anymore. I truly appreciate his taking time out of his busy schedule to review the manuscript and write a foreword.

I'm thankful for Dr. Fred Adrian who looked after me during a brief hospital stay not long ago. During that time he encouraged me by showing an interest in my writing and he provided material that is now part of the book.

I thank Dr. Phillip Long, my current doctor, who has given me such tremendous support over the past few years. With his help in finding effective medications, I got through a difficult period and became well enough to finish this work.

I'm grateful to Fred Hizsa and Lori Jensen Gwynne, two friends who were very helpful in providing feedback and editing for *Riding the Roller Coaster* in its beginning stages. Thank you, Fred, for keeping me on track by pointing out that this book was not the place to share my favorite recipes. And I'll never forget the morning that Lori, an accomplished writer and editor, sat me down after reading the entire draft in one sitting and filled me in on some of the basic mistakes I was making with words, grammar, and punctuation. Thanks, Lori, for all your encouragement.

A big thank you to the Port Moody Writer's Workshop which provided wonderful weekly meetings where I learned more about writing and received helpful critiques on some of the "Roller Coaster" essays. Eileen Kernaghan, the leader of the workshop, is such a gem of a teacher, never tiring of sharing her bounty of knowledge.

Thanks also to Pastor Tineke Rijzinga for the comfort she gave me at a time when I needed it badly. Her eager reaction to the book project gave me a real boost.

I'm very grateful to Pastor Dale Cuming and his wife, Marlene, for always being there when I needed to talk – and a lot of talking I did at times! What a comfort it was to have warm-hearted folk like that to turn to when I was in trouble! Their example and guidance as well as the care and love of the rest of my church family help remind me that God is always there.

When I began writing about mood disorders – about all the anger I felt at how the world misunderstands those of us with mental illnesses – I worked alone. I didn't realize that there were organizations that had the same goals as I did: to inform the public and reduce the stigma. The writing was tough; I didn't know where to start or where to direct the writing.

I was so happy when I found the Mood Disorders Association of B.C. and Robert Winram, its executive director. Robert has been a good friend to me and a very big support. I've often faxed him pieces of writing I had problems with and he never tired of offering help by suggesting changes where needed. His self-help groups meet regularly – a welcome place to go when I need to be with people who will understand me. Thank you so much, Robert!

I am grateful for the Canadian Mental Health Association (the B.C. Division and Vancouver-Burnaby Branch). Executive director Bev Gutray of the B.C. Division has been very encouraging. I'll never forget the first time I met Bev and we discussed the needs of the mentally ill. I walked out of her office with a briefcase bulging with reading material. She was so eager to have me understand the issues; and I was excited to have found an organization that treated me seriously and was willing to involve me in some way.

Later I met Andrea Porter (also from the B.C. Division) who engaged me in several CMHA projects. I remember fondly the time I talked to Andrea about an idea I had to create church bulletins celebrating Mental Health Awareness Week. Almost immediately she asked me, "Do you want to do it?" And before I realized it I was working on – what was to me – a dream project. Thank you, Andrea!

When I look back at that first time I struggled so hard to express in writing what I had been through and what I knew many thousands of others were going through, I can honestly say that *Riding the Roller Coaster* could not have been completed without the support of Robert, Bev, and Andrea and their organizations. They showed me that it's not only okay to talk about mental illness, but it's of utmost importance to do so. It's only in this way that we can increase the public's awareness and begin to make the world a better place for those who have for too long been misunderstood.

In conclusion I want to offer a big thank you to Northstone Publishing and Mike Schwartzentruber for making the publication of *Riding the Roller Coaster* a reality. I'm so glad to have found a publisher like you.

Foreword

It is an honor to have been asked by Marja Bergen to provide a foreword to this most remarkable volume, wherein she shares her personal experience of everyday living with a complex mental disorder. Throughout *Riding the Roller Coaster*, she offers practical suggestions and strategies for overcoming the difficulties she, like so many others, experiences. Many persons will identify with the moods, thoughts, and experiences she recounts in this book. Essentially, Marja offers encouragement and understanding to those individuals who suffer conditions we call mental illnesses. In her creative way, she demonstrates how a person can successfully ride the roller coaster of relapses and remissions which typify these conditions.

Someone observing Marja's life may wonder what factors have influenced her success – and she *has* had an extremely constructive and productive life. Certainly, Marja's experience has been enhanced by a very supportive husband and the fulfillment of being a mother to a wonderful son. Marja also expresses her creativity, not only through her writing, but through her work as a gifted photographer, as a cookbook author, and as an advocate for others who suffer similar afflictions.

Throughout the volume we become aware of Marja's vulnerability to stress – a challenge faced by so many of those with mental illnesses who have a particular need to deal with, and to receive appropriate assistance in dealing with, the stressful parts of their lives. Marja, with her insightful understanding, takes a positive approach by making the most of the well times. She also includes practical examples of how to develop mastery over times which are dark and distressing through the maintenance of hope and purposeful activity.

Marja has many basic strengths which have always included hopefulness. Nevertheless, she has at times needed to reach out to others for support and encouragement. Acknowledging her needs, she has tried to remain in a supportive, continuous therapeutic relationship, which has given her some protection from periods of relapse. Even though her treatments did not always successfully alleviate her symptoms or reduce her pain, she always went for further guidance and support concerning medications and therapeutic strategies. She has also been extremely conscientious in taking her medications on a regular basis, despite their limitations and at times their failure, to help her deal with her thoughts and emotions.

Marja has recognized and tried to conquer the stigma of mental illness within herself and within her family, dealing with this in a positive advocacy role with other people and organizations.

Many years ago, one of my supervisors, Dr. William Murphy of Boston, recommended maintaining contact with one's patients as a way of continuing the relationship. Marja and I have stayed in contact for the past 30 years. One of the most gratifying parts of a physician's professional life is knowing and working with a person like her. I have been in awe of Marja's many talents and her creativity in photography and writing. It has been an honor to have known her over these past many years.

Marja's nurturing approach, positive outlook, and enduring faith will be a particularly helpful example for many people.

Gerald M. McDougall, MD, FRPCP

Introduction

This book is written for those who share with me the struggles of living with a mental illness. In these pages, I would like to share what I've learned after living with manic depression and psychosis for 30 years. Over these years I have gradually adopted a lifestyle that makes it possible not only to cope, but to live a full and productive life.

The skills I will discuss can benefit all people, but for those who have a mental illness, whether it be anxiety, depression (unipolar), manic depression (bipolar), or even schizophrenia, they are especially important.

First, however, I should explain that over the years I have received a variety of diagnoses from different doctors. Mental illnesses such as mood disorders and schizophrenia often have overlapping symptoms. Both are complex in nature and many cases are hard to pigeonhole. At times I may have exhibited more symptoms of one condition than another. Having been a fairly "compliant" patient, I've taken medication constantly for many years, no doubt hiding many clues that might have made diagnosis easier.

Most recently, the doctors have been very definite in their opinion that I have a bipolar illness and I am successfully treated on that basis.

Still, I am not always well. I have problems like anyone who lives with an illness such as this. Although I function normally much of the time, symptoms often arise. I could not live without medications. But I've found that medications alone are not all we need. It is also important to take control of our lives by maintaining a healthy lifestyle with positive attitudes.

Learning to live with a mood disorder is something we begin to do gradually, as our life unfolds. Bit by bit we get to know what our illness does to us and we become able to recognize the symptoms before they cause severe problems. As we get older we grow in our ability to manage the illness better. There is much we can do to develop a life we can call successful: Yes – even *with* a mental illness!

Good medical care is the most important thing to start with. When we find a doctor who prescribes medications that work well for us we have the major tool to start building a healthy life. But relying on a doctor's help and taking pills, although very necessary, must not be considered the only treatment possible. This treatment is passive in nature – it's something that's being done for us and does nothing to take us out of the victim role. To become *really* well, we need to take an active part in improving our lives. Taking control and making things happen *for* us is far better than waiting for something to happen *to* us.

Life can hold rich possibilities. Some of the main obstacles in our way are our attitudes – toward ourselves, our illness, and our potential. In my view the stigma attached to mental illness is the worst culprit in reducing self-esteem. We can overcome the effects of this stigma by accepting the fact that our illness is an illness like any other. There is nothing to be ashamed of. I know from experience that, if we can accept this, our confidence will increase dramatically and we will be able to pursue a life filled with meaningful goals.

I've focused to a high degree on the role of creativity in keeping us well. My own life has been dramatically affected by creative activity and I know there are great benefits to be gained from it. Doing photography for many years gave me a feeling of ability, satisfaction, and recognition from others. This in turn built my self-esteem and confidence. I became part of a community of photographers and received a feeling of belonging.

Likewise I've gained feelings of accomplishment from needlework, cooking, and self-publishing cookbooks. The projects I engaged in made it exciting to get up in the morning. Seeing the hours stretch ahead was much like sitting down to a banquet table filled with delicious foods – foods of many colors and flavors. Yes, having a creative urge *is* valuable. It's available to everyone, yet so many people have not explored what's possible for them.

I know that I'm a fortunate person who has had much support from my husband. The pressure to work at a paying job has not been as great for me as it is for most.

I've ended up a stay-at-home mother and wife who found happiness and a sense of usefulness in doing volunteer work as well as working on the creative projects that I loved so much. Writing this book is one of the products of this freedom I've had.

Over the two years it took me to write this book, I went through a myriad of mood changes. It was not a stable period for me. Some of the essays may seem as though they were written by another person. But they're all mine, someone who was experiencing the fluctuations of her moods. Often I wondered what I was doing writing a book such as this. Was I qualified? But, as so often happens with the hardships we endure, I was able to glean an understanding that I can now pass on to others.

One caution before you start reading: In this book I've described how *I* am affected by this illness. Others may find that their own stories would be quite different. Each of us is unique and experiences life in his or her own way. Much depends on our personality, our environment, our circumstances, and the kind of support we receive. Although the basic symptoms are similar, they vary in how they manifest themselves in each of our lives.

If you are only beginning your journey with mental illness, it is my sincere hope that this book will help you realize that this doesn't have to mean "the end of the world" for you. There *is* a way to take charge of your well-being and to discover the many possibilities life holds for you.

1

WHAT IS A
MOOD DISORDER?

What is a Mood Disorder?

*Life is a fever-dream made up of joys embittered by sorrows, pleasure
poisoned by pain; a dream that is
a nightmare-confusion of spasmodic and fleeting delights, ecstasies,
exaltations, happinesses, interspersed with
long-drawn miseries, griefs, perils, horrors,
disappointments and despairs...*
– Mark Twain

Our moods dictate how we feel about the world. They determine our attitudes toward life. They have an effect on how we handle lifestyles and whether or not we find fulfillment. When moods reach extremes, as they do in people with depression and manic depression, lives can be affected in a dramatic way.

Today, most experts believe that mood disorders (or affective disorders) have a physical basis which can usually be treated effectively with medication. Something happens to the chemistry in the brain which impairs the ability of thought messages to pass as they should from one area to another. The resulting interruption of the process can cause a mood disturbance, as well as loss of memory and misperception of reality.

There are two major kinds of emotional states involved in mood disorders: depression and mania. Those who have a unipolar mood disorder experience frequent bouts of depression. Those with a bipolar mood disorder (or manic depression) experience mood swings which bring them up to euphoric heights and then crash them down into deep lows. Often there are well periods between these extremes; other times they swing back and forth from one to the other.

These moods affect our feeling, thinking, and behavior. We are usually unaware of what's happening. Often we don't see what has happened to us until our illness has advanced so far that the situation has become critical.

After living with the illness a long time, some of us gradually learn to listen to our friends and family when they warn us that we are heading for trouble. As we learn to live with our moods it becomes more likely that we will know the warning signs as they develop. The ability to recognize these symptoms provides a valuable tool for avoiding serious problems.

Depression

It is a time when one's spirit is subdued and sad, one knows not why;
when the past seems a storm-swept desolation, life a vanity and a burden,
and the future but a way to death.
– Mark Twain, *The Gilded Age*

Depression often creeps up without our knowing it. One day we suddenly realize that we're not really happy anymore; we always feel tired; life no longer has the sparkle it used to have.

For many of us depression can become so severe that it's a struggle to move out of the bedroom. We want to be by ourselves; we cannot cope with the people and activity outside.

For a few of us a form of paralysis sets in. It becomes almost impossible to speak, eat, or dress ourselves.

Symptoms of Depression

- We become trapped in negative thinking which leads to feelings of guilt, hopelessness, and worthlessness.
- We notice a marked decrease in interest in hobbies and in activities we usually enjoy.
- We experience an increase or decrease in appetite resulting in weight gain or loss.
- We experience a disruption of sleeping habits; we are unable to get to sleep at night and wake too early in the morning; or we sleep more than usual.
- We move more slowly than usual.
- We are unable to concentrate well – reading becomes difficult.
- We become forgetful.
- We have difficulty making decisions.
- We are plagued by thoughts of death and suicide.
- We suffer a loss of confidence and self-esteem.
- We become agitated or restless so that we can't keep still.
- We experience decreased sex drive.
- We use excessive amounts of alcohol and/or nonprescription drugs.
- We suffer from fatigue or loss of energy.

If we persistently experience some of these symptoms, or when our usual functioning has been impaired by these symptoms, we have a depressive disorder, a disorder that can in most cases be treated.

Some people think that depression is the same as sadness. But, in my eyes, there's actually quite a difference between the two.

Many times, when I feel sad, I cry. It feels good to be able to express myself this way. I think that feeling anything is actually a good thing – whether it's joy or sadness. It's all part of belonging to humanity in what is often a humorous, but even more often, a tragic world.

But sometimes, when all I feel is a deep dark nothing – when I can't laugh or cry – at times like this I'm experiencing depression at its worst.

There's no emotion to this mood – no moving of the spirit – it's static. The shadow of a kind of paralysis sets in. It's difficult at times like this to believe there's anything more to life than this. It seems as though there's no way out of the emptiness.

Mania

I raced about like a crazed weasel, bubbling with plans and enthusiasm,
immersed in sports,
and staying up all night, night after night.
– Kay Redfield Jamison, *An Unquiet Mind*

For those with a bipolar disorder, mania, the opposite extreme of depression, can also creep up and catch us unawares. Our mood becomes elated; life looks great. In the beginning stages we appear to be more self-confident, perceptive, and creative than usual.

Symptoms of Mania

- We have more energy than we're able to keep up with. We move from one activity to another without stopping.
- Our thoughts come quickly and fluently. Our mind races, jumping from one topic to another. We speak rapidly.
- We become extremely irritable.

- We experience unpredictable emotional changes.
- We overspend and give money away freely; we go on buying sprees and incur heavy debts.
- We experience inflated self-esteem and believe we can do almost anything.
- We have a decreased need for sleep – even believing that we don't need sleep.
- We experience increased sex drive and may fall victim to sexual indiscretions and indiscriminate picking of sexual partners.
- We show poor judgment.
- We become easily distracted by unimportant or irrelevant things.

For many, this manic mood is the most dangerous of the two extremes. It is common not to recognize that we have an illness (denial) and to refuse treatment. Mania can be destructive to our relationships, to our reputation, and to our finances. This mood often causes permanent damage in our lives.

A Case of Hypomania

Husband Wes and son Jeff came home yesterday. Their idyllic father-and-son outing to Oregon via a Cessna 172, piloted by Wes himself, had ground to a crashing halt when the plane ran into vicious turbulence while landing and hit some trees. The plane was a write-off but miraculously both of them survived, literally walking away from the scene. The worst injuries were a minor nose fracture for Jeff, and a cracked rib and broken collarbone for Wes.

I had been depressed for many months, often dazed, confused, and disorganized. But on hearing the news of their accident and how they survived, something clicked. It was as if this nearly tragic event triggered something in my head, much like a mild dose of shock treatment. A moderately high mood (or hypomania) developed. My mind and body became ready to respond to someone else's need. I became energetic, focusing on what had to be done, my own problems no longer on my mind.

Wes and Jeff didn't really need me much when they arrived home. Nevertheless, the little I did for them truly helped awaken me from the sleep my spirit had been in for so long.

Within two or three days my fresh energy caused my mind to become actively involved making plans. Around and around in my head, I rolled over the ideas for the following projects. I wanted to begin to do all these as soon as possible:

- redo a family cookbook I had edited, to make it suitable for the market,
- coordinate the production of another cookbook,
- buy a new sofa,
- replace the computer desk in the bedroom with a bookcase,
- tidy up the three horribly messy rooms in the house, and
- take on a Sunday School class.

I *almost* bought an expensive pair of shoes without thinking it over first. (Lucky for Wes impulse buying has not been one of my problems.)

Everything I wanted to do seemed possible. Chores I usually dreaded actually became enjoyable.

I became unusually talkative, eager to tell family and friends about all my plans. I wanted to write. For the first time in months I wanted to dust off my camera and make photographs again.

The good that developed from this new activity in my mind was that I actually did some of the things I had planned. I rearranged some of the furniture which helped me organize my books, photographs, and papers better.

And (lo and behold!) I cleaned up two rooms, throwing away mountains of long-collected stuff: things that we hadn't looked at for the past 20 years; things we would probably never look at again for the next 20 years.

I was in the mood to do extras in the kitchen, baking not because company was coming, but simply because I felt like it.

As the weeks went by my mood gradually became more normal. I remained active, yet not overly so. And the depression that had plagued me had disappeared.

Note: My doctor had started me on a new anti-psychotic drug. This was undoubtedly part of the reason my mood changed for the better. Yet the shock of nearly losing my husband and son seemed to help it kick in.

Psychosis

I believed I could stop cars and paralyze their forces by
merely standing in the middle of the highway with my arms outspread...
I suspected I was a reincarnation of the Holy Ghost...
– Robert Lowell, *Robert Lowell* by Hamilton

Some people with manic depression become psychotic if the mania is left untreated for too long. At its worst the pieces of our world come together in grotesque and alien patterns. Our life becomes a nightmare from which we feel we can't escape. There are anti-psychotic medications that can successfully treat this condition.

Symptoms of Psychosis

- We can't distinguish reality from fantasy.
- Sometimes we imagine we are a religious figure, that we are able to save the world from evil forces, or that we are directed by a superior power (delusion).
- We feel threatened or feel there are plots against us, often by people who are close to us (paranoia).
- We see, hear, or smell things that are not real (hallucination).

These symptoms resemble those of schizophrenia but they can be present in severe cases of manic depression as well. As long as we go for help, get treatment in the form of medication, and follow a doctor's orders for taking them, these symptoms shouldn't continue for long.

Nights of Psychosis

Memories of my first illness, a severe psychosis, sometimes come pouring back into my mind.

I remember that rainy night I got lost when I was to meet my sister downtown...becoming disoriented...walking in the midst of a dazzle of lights and a myriad of shoppers...unconscious as if in a dream...waking up some time later (was it 5 or 20 minutes that went by?)...not recognizing where I was...only seeing that I'd walked to a place I didn't recognize...all around me people rushing and neon blinding, their crazed reflections on the black wet pavement... Lost.

Walking to the bus stop I had felt as if a slow-moving taxicab driving alongside was following me. I was convinced that the driver was waiting for a chance to stop and grab me...sent by the men who were plotting my death.

My growing paranoid panic drove me to run up the front steps of a well-lit house. I knocked feverishly on the door. Soon a man and woman opened it. "I'm being followed," I gasped, "Someone is trying to kidnap me! Please call the police!" Some time later the kind couple drove me to the nearby bus depot. It was a short relief in a long night filled with terror, one of many such nights.

Was it that same night that I sat on a bus, safely on the seat behind the driver, believing that he would somehow protect me from the danger outside?... And every time the bus stopped and the doors opened...I saw a man in the dark...on the sidewalk outside...wearing a raincoat...hands in his pockets...hands clutching hidden guns... And the doors clapping shut...and the bus driving on into the rainy night...on to the next stop...on to where another stranger waited...hands in his pockets...threatening... At every stop another danger... At every stop another flood of fear.

Within my mind lived the delusion that I knew of an underground movement which was plotting to destroy the world. In my confusion I believed that I was the only one aware of this plot and that those involved thought I would tell authorities about it. The fear of danger was always with me but in the dark of night it was at its worst.

On one of these nights my sister and I were drawn by the light coming from the open doors of a church basement. There was a fall fair in progress. We decided to go in. As we wandered past the booths, menacing faces, ugly and evil, stared out at me – much like the stone gargoyles of a Gothic cathedral. There was no peace or safety anywhere. The constant fear exhausted me.

Back home I wandered from room to room...talking nonsensically of the evils of money...emptying my pockets of change...throwing dimes and quarters into the kitchen garbage pail.

I remember the hours of manic typing on Dad's old Remington, typing an inspired but insane flow of words; then taking my precious bundle of papers to the newspaper office and daring – demanding – the editors to publish what I'd written. I felt that what I had written was important, although in what way I don't know. All I know is that this was what I was driven to do.

These were the nights when I paced endlessly around and around the living room, possessed with racing thoughts, thoughts that I could not escape.

These were the sleepless nights, the nights I heard rustling noises outside, believing the men with the guns were out there. Fear gripped every part of my physical and mental being.

And so the memories of these terror-filled days and nights melt together – memories of one long nightmare from which it had seemed I would never waken.

A Roller-Coaster Ride

They mount up to the heaven, they go down again to the depths.
– Psalm 107:26

When those of us with manic depression have been high for a while, a time will come when we will finally drop down again. If we don't fall too far we may achieve what could be considered a normal mood. This may last for a time, but often we will sense the loss of elation we had become accustomed to and we will become depressed. We might crash even further, directly into a deep depression. It seems that the higher we are, the lower we're likely to fall. This is a good reason for not allowing our moods to pass too far beyond normal. It's best to see a doctor early.

When we're depressed we may get to the point where our mood lifts, giving way to a sudden brightening of our spirits. This feeling can gradually rise to a full mania, eventually to return to depression. And so our lives take us from despair to elation and then back down again on what seems like a constant roller-coaster ride.

Mood-stabilizing medications such as lithium are now able to reduce these ups and downs significantly; they can allow us to live close-to-normal lives. We can help avoid the unnecessary pain of mood swings by leading a balanced and healthy lifestyle and by not overdoing things.

Patterns of Bipolar Disorder

Bipolar disorder has many variations. The length, frequency, and pattern of episodes differs from one person to another.

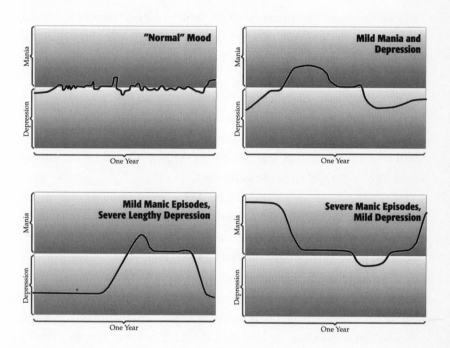

Keeping a Balance

Give me a firm place to stand, and I will move the earth.
– Archimedes (c.287–212 BC)

The day-to-day life of a person with unipolar or bipolar disorder is, under stable conditions and with effective medication, not so different from the life of a healthy person. Many of us have jobs and take part in leisure activities the way anyone would.

Problems arise though, even in those who are well treated, when a number of stressful events come together. Everyone has *some* difficulty with stressful times, but when those of us with a mood disorder undergo stress, whether it's good or bad, our stability is thrown off and our treatment might have to be altered to see us through.

We may become depressed or high. Whichever mood we're in might last a few days or a few months. Everyone's experiences differ from those others have; and each time we experience a mood swing, the way it manifests itself will probably never be exactly the same.

If we recognize the symptoms early and see a doctor to review medications, chances that the mood will persist will be greatly reduced. And if we can manage to bounce back quickly, chances of severe future attacks are lessened.

The best way to live our lives is to avoid a lot of unnecessary stress by trying to keep a balance – by not planning too many exciting activities at once, by leaving sufficient time to be quietly by ourselves with some freedom to "do our own thing." Everyone needs time to relax.

If we plan our days well, with a variety of activities, especially if we include some that will bring us enjoyment and satisfaction, the chances of having stability in our lives are optimized.

Beyond the Moment

It's odd how I never seem to learn. When profound emotion strikes – whether it be sadness, joy, emptiness, or pain – it always seems as though that feeling is going to last forever. At times it's almost unthinkable that the mood I have at the moment could ever change.

When I feel lonely, I feel like I've always been lonely in the past and will always be lonely in the future. It's as though I'm wearing blinders and I can't see beyond this point in time.

When I'm overjoyed with life, feeling fortunate and confident, it would be hard to convince me that things might be quite different tomorrow.

It seems that it's part of our nature not to be able to see what feelings are possible for us beyond the "now." I *do* understand that moods fluctuate, and that often there's no really good reason for it. I know that – and yet it's so easy to forget.

My Rainbow

When the cloud is scattered
The rainbow's glory is shed.
– Percy Bysshe Shelley, *When the Lamp Is Shattered*

One of the things I don't mind about having a bipolar disorder is that it's provided me with a veritable rainbow of feelings. A rich assortment of feelings and moods is ever-present in my day-to-day life. The "colors" range from joyful to painfully sad, but I've learned to value many of them.

Everyone has feelings, but I believe that people with my illness tend to sense things more strongly than many because our moods go up and down to such an intense degree. In a way it's good to be able to feel strongly: to know what it is to be swept away by beautiful music, to be deeply touched by a friend's words, and to sense fully the excitement of doing creative things.

It may seem strange, but I even value being able to feel sorrow deeply. What if I weren't able to feel? What if I were like a stone – insensitive? There is a richness to a heart that can contain truly deep feelings – in laughter *and* in tears. When I feel strongly, I sense my humanity intensely.

I am happy and grateful that I have a brilliant rainbow inside me. I know that *all* the colors – from blue to green to yellow and red – are necessary to make it what it is. Although some of its hues may be painful to me, the arch, in its entirety, is a wondrous phenomenon and the beautiful part of a storm.

An Illness Like Any Other

What consoles me is that I am beginning to consider madness as an
illness like any other, and that I accept it as such.
– Vincent van Gogh, in a letter to Theo, his brother, 1889

We always think of mental illness as something that happens to other people, not to us. To be diagnosed with depression or manic depression is a scary thing. But how we cope with our mood disorder is largely determined by how we look at it. If we can accept it as the illness it is – an illness like any other – we will be ready to move ahead with our lives in a positive way.

The negative view much of society has of mental disorders is partly due to the fact that people do not understand there is usually a physical basis for these illnesses, often in the form of a chemical imbalance. This imbalance is treatable with medication. With effective treatment most of us can live close-to-normal lives. Mental illness *is* an illness like any other.

In fact, mood disorders are comparable to other illnesses, such as diabetes. A diabetic is not to blame for his or her illness. Neither is a person with a mood disorder. Just as diabetes can cause serious disability and even death, so too can mood disorders. Diabetics often require the use of medication to maintain stable blood sugar levels. People with mood disorders also require medications, in their case, to maintain emotional balance. Finally, as is the case with those who have diabetes, if people with mood disorders take their medications regularly, chances are they will live a close-to-normal life.

Nevertheless, because of the fear of having a "shameful" condition, or of being labeled by society, many don't search out the help they so desperately need. What results is much unnecessary suffering by people who could otherwise have been helped.

In recent years much research has been done and doctors, mental health associations, societies, and libraries can provide much information. Mood disorder self-support groups are an especially good source of information. Here we can find pertinent literature and discuss affective illnesses with others who have problems similar to our own. (More about self-help support groups on page 93.)

As we come to terms with our disease we learn to understand how imperative medications and other treatments are – how they form the basis for our well-being. Once we have the physical aspects of our illness under control, we can prepare to take charge of our lives and make the most of the strengths we all have.

As we walk with our friends and acquaintances, we should walk with self-assurance. In that great family of individuals who suffer from personal problems, sicknesses, and handicaps, each of us is a unique yet ordinary member.

Dealing With the Stigma

*Mental illness is so common that if even a small proportion of
the patients made a special effort to learn as much as they could about their
illness, and if they proceeded to educate their families and friends, there
would not be too many uninformed people left and the stigma
associated with mental illness would be virtually eradicated.*
– Dr. John Varsamis, M.D.,
Society for Depression & Manic Depression of Manitoba Newsletter, April 1990

Society has historically had a negative, unsympathetic view of people with mental illness. This is mainly due to the failure to recognize it as the biochemical sickness it is. Some people tend to think of our disorder as a character flaw, as a hopeless condition.

If people could only know us as the individuals we are, individuals with sensitivity like anyone else. If they could only see past the labels they put on us. If they would only realize that we desire the same from life as they do. We too need love and acceptance, and want to make a contribution to the community we live in. We are human beings, not simply the faceless, sensationalized cases people read about in the newspapers.

Yet there is much we ourselves can do to remove the stigma which has so long been attached to illnesses such as ours. Society is not the only one to blame. Too many of us needlessly keep our illness secret, even from close friends. The shame we feel, because of the branding, presents the major problem and the branding tends to be caused by this feeling of shame. Someone, somehow, must break this vicious cycle. As Dr. Varsamis suggests above, we, the people who experience the disease first hand, are the best candidates to do this. If we could learn all we can about our illness from our doctors, from books and support groups and mental health organizations, we would be in a good position to educate others. What's more, by the time we ourselves have become fully informed about our disorder, we'll find that there really is no justification for the stigma – no need to be ashamed.

When we feel good about who we are, it becomes possible to talk to our acquaintances about our illness in a matter-of-fact way. How we view our condition and the attitude with which we reveal it to others will help determine how others will view us. Chances are that our friends will be surprised and curious to know more. We will have an opportunity to explain mood disorders. This would help them to understand us and, in a small way, would help our community's understanding to grow. What's more, we could have a new ally, someone who might very well be sympathetic and supportive.

There was a time, not long ago, when people with cancer were whispered about. There was shame attached to having the illness. "Cancer" was a dirty word. But things are different now. Cancer research is generously supported by the community. The illness is openly discussed. A new, sympathetic view should be possible for those suffering with mental illness as well.

One day, when enough of us have spoken out, there *will* be less stigma. The community will be more prepared to open their hearts and give care and support to those with mental illnesses. We will no longer be alone in our suffering.

No One Brought Me Flowers

Long ago, at the age of 19, I became very sick. I was in hospital for ten months. But no one gave me flowers or sent me get-well cards. I received few visitors. This is because I had a mental illness at a time when there was much less understanding, an illness many people thought of as shameful.

They didn't say in so many words that it was something to be ashamed of, but their unwillingness to discuss it and the tendency to hide its existence suggested it. Some people felt illnesses of the mind were brought on by the patients themselves. They felt sheer will power could overcome it.

But I did try; I tried very hard to get better. Each morning I got up and joined the other patients in the terrazzo-floored institutional bathroom. I slowly and carefully washed my face and combed my long hair. The night's rest had cleared my mind and I felt ready to face a new day – ready to try again.

But, invariably, an hour later at breakfast, my nightmare once again took control. I shut the blinds, fearfully hiding from the men with the rifles who I imagined were out there, waiting to shoot me. These thoughts formed my reality; the chemistry in my brain had deranged my mind.

I was a frightened girl, spending most of my mornings marching up and down the long hallway, well away from the windows, away from the eyes of the wicked men with the guns. I bravely sang Onward Christian Soldiers, not because I was a Christian but because I believed the louder I sang, the more I taunted my enemies, proving to them that I was not afraid. Singing the old gospel hymn gave me courage, a sense of power and strength.

It was a very scary thing to be committed to an institution like this. I was so young. I hadn't done anything wrong.

But now I was someone who was whispered about and wondered about. My sickness was not an acceptable one. I suffered so very much. But no one brought me flowers.

Anger Diffused

I had, for such a long time, been so terribly angry – angry at how the world seems to treat people with illnesses like mine. I know that I am an okay person. I have friends; I do things other people do; I want to make contributions to the world like most people do. I'm not so different.

The only thing is that my brain often works differently from other people's. I try my best to be like others, but often, without knowing it, I act differently, strangely, or even rudely – in a way that doesn't fit with how others behave. Often I don't realize how my behavior looks to others until much later. Then I really suffer. I feel so bad that, sometimes, I wake in the middle of the night remembering what I have done – kicking myself and cursing.

Yet this illness is not something I can always control. I can't help that I've ended up with manic depression. It could happen to anyone.

And yet I hear people talk about "madness" and "the nuts at the funny farm." That hurts a lot.

Yes, up until a few years ago I used to get very angry about this injustice. But I have begun to write about the feelings I have as one who has a mental illness – for newspapers, newsletters, a magazine, and now this book. I've been very open about this. Thanks to this "coming out of the closet" I don't feel the anger nearly so much. Through my writing, friends and acquaintances have learned that I have a mood disorder – yet I have found that, except for a few cases, this honesty hasn't hurt me too much.

At church, in particular, people are very understanding. When they ask me how I'm doing, they really seem to want to know. If I tell them that I'm not too well, they know what I'm talking about – and they're always ready with a hug when I need it.

I've learned, though, that I shouldn't dwell on my problems when with friends. There are so many other things to talk about, so many other things to do. I know that not everyone can afford to be as honest as I've been. Most people need jobs – and employers are not always so understanding. But maybe one day this will change. Maybe one day the world will understand and accept mental illnesses as they do other illnesses. Maybe the generations that follow ours won't have to fear the shame that so many of us do today.

2

GETTING HELP

Denial

There should be no shame in becoming mentally ill.
We need to break this fearful silence
that has kept people from coming for help.
– Robert Winram, *The Vancouver Province*, May 7, 1993

Too many of us refuse to face the fact that there is something wrong with us. We are so afraid of having a mental illness that we pretend everything is fine. Most of the time we just can't recognize that the way we behave, think, and feel is not as it should be.

Friends and family may suggest to us that we have a problem and should get help. But we create arguments, trying desperately to prove them wrong. We refuse to see our true circumstances. And so we continue to suffer, together with the loved ones who have to live with us.

Denial is costly. It prevents us from facing the problem and from learning about the illness and getting treatment. Tragically, denial can cause some people years of unhappiness and lack of fulfillment. Effective medications could have put them back on the road to a good, full life.

Modern medicine offers a lot that can help us once we are willing to accept the presence of an illness. Psychotherapy, medication, and support groups can help us deal with it and make us well. When we face the truth about our mental health our lives can begin to improve.

Getting Help

In great straits, and when hope is small,
the boldest counsels are the safest.
– Livy (59 BC–17 AD)

When we become familiar with the signs of depression or mania (see pages 20 and 21) and they become evident, when normal life becomes difficult, it is vital to seek help. To wait would mean that we could become sicker. Medical treatments work best when the symptoms are not too advanced. We need to let our doctor know when our moods are becoming abnormal.

A doctor is the only one who should advise us whether to alter our medications. We should not attempt to self-medicate.

In a crisis situation (when we're dangerously high or so low that we want to die) it is best to find a close friend or family member to come to the doctor's office or emergency ward with us. It will feel better to have the support. This person can get us there safely and help explain things.

If the doctor's office is open, it would be best to see him or her first. The doctor can assess whether hospitalization will be necessary. When the doctor's office is closed, go to the emergency ward at the hospital. If possible, go to a hospital where your doctor has privileges and where your records are on file. If you're admitted to hospital, the staff will be able to monitor your progress as you work at getting better.

Remember, a mood disorder is an illness like any other and, if we are to recover, we need treatment. We have to have the good sense to get assistance. We may even have to allow others to have that good sense for us. There is hope for those who do seek help; most of us will get our health back and be able to lead a good life.

Medications

If you do not hope, you will not find what is beyond your hopes.
– St. Clement of Alexandria, *Stromateis*

Psychiatry is a relatively new medical field. Psychiatric medications only came into use in the 1950s. Since that time there have been great advancements with many drugs now available for doctors to choose from. It's truly exciting to see how many options doctors have for treating us today.

There are four major groups of medications available for our use, depending on our symptoms and needs. The basic categories are anti-anxiety drugs, anti-psychotic drugs, antidepressants, and mood stabilizers.

Everyone responds differently to medications. We may respond to several or to only one or two. During our treatment we must be prepared to experiment until we find something that works for us. We should not do this on our own, of course, but trust our doctor's expertise in the prescribing.

Unfortunately, most medications *do* have side effects – some more than others. Medications can cause weight gain or appetite loss, constipation or diarrhea, drowsiness or insomnia, and many other side effects, depending on what the medication is and who's taking it. For many people, the side effects are not severe at all. But for others it may become necessary to weigh the drawbacks against the benefits. If the side effects are too hard to bear, we might need to take another drug to counteract them.

Sometimes it becomes difficult to keep track of the medications we take. We may forget to take our pills. Drug stores sell the perfect answer to this problem: pill dispensers which are divided into compartments. There is a box for a day's use, with four compartments for different times of the day. Another box is for a full week's use, with compartments for each day. These dispensers can ensure that we remember to take our pills regularly.

Some words about managing our medicine cabinet: For safety and to avoid confusion, we should always throw away old medications when we're not using them anymore. (Return them to your pharmacist.) When we're depressed, it would be wise to keep only small supplies of medication at home, letting a friend or family member keep the rest temporarily.

When undergoing an adjustment to our medications, we should not expect that we will experience improvement immediately. Most psychiatric drugs take a few weeks to kick in. A few begin to work almost immediately in some people, but can take up to six weeks to work in others. It's important to be patient and to give it a fair chance.

It's unfortunate that many people with mood disorders are ashamed of their need for medications and resist taking them. Erroneously, they don't look on their problem as a medical one. They haven't yet recognized that their illness has a biochemical basis. We must realize that, in the same way as people with diabetes or heart disease need medication to survive, we who have mood disorders require treatment as well.

Coming to Terms With Pills

When I was young and just learning to live with my bipolar mood disorder, I often stopped taking my medication. Each time I started feeling better I assumed my illness was beaten – gone for good – and I would stop taking my pills. I didn't realize that my problems would probably be with me all my life and that I would need medications indefinitely.

Each time I stopped taking my pills I became sick again. It took a number of years before I was able to put two and two together and to realize that I would always need medication if I were to live a normal life.

Today I wouldn't think of going without my pills – I know that the chemistry of my brain needs them to function normally. It will probably always be this way for me. I accept this now, take my pills (religiously), and, except for occasional problems, lead a close-to-normal life.

Psychotherapy

To whom can I speak today? I am heavy-laden with trouble...
– The Man Who Was Tired of Life (c.1990 BC)

It would be difficult (and unwise) to live with a mood disorder and not see a psychiatrist or therapist. We need a doctor to diagnose our problem, prescribe medication, and to talk to about our thoughts and feelings. The talking part of our treatment is called psychotherapy.

Sigmund Freud was the first psychoanalyst. When he tried to use his talk therapy on people with mood disorders, he found that he did not have the good results he had from patients with other disorders. It has since been found that, in severe forms of depression and manic depression, simply having patients discuss their thoughts is not helpful; medications, *combined with* talk therapy, produce the best response.

One form of treatment is cognitive therapy. An activity-oriented therapy, it focuses on behavior, perception, and beliefs. The doctor steers the patient away from negative beliefs toward a more realistic appraisal of the world. This treatment has proven very successful.

Cognitive therapy is primarily useful for those with a unipolar disorder, but it can be used as an adjunct to medication for those with a bipolar disorder. Even if we see a doctor who does not use a specialized technique, having a professional to talk to on a regular basis is important to everyone with mood disorders. Our ups and downs often present problems which we need to discuss. Talking things out once a month or so is reassuring. Our doctor can help us recognize symptoms we didn't realize we had. He or she can make suggestions for adjusting our medications when necessary. A professional whom we feel comfortable with can be our most valuable ally in our effort to be well.

An Important Visit

I see my doctor about every two months. This is not necessarily because I'm not well. I need these visits because, invariably over the 60-day period, much happens that I need to talk about: things that frustrate me or hurt me, things I'm doing that I'm excited about and just have to talk about. Often I have symptoms we need to discuss. He reviews my medications and determines whether they need to be changed.

Talking to my doctor, who has come to know me so well and who is so understanding, is an outlet I very much need. There's no friend I could talk to in quite the same way. It's good to have a professional listen and respond to how my life is going. He encourages me and helps me get a fresh perspective on things when I need it.

When I get up to leave, I feel prepared to face another 60 days.

Finding a Good Doctor

So many men, so many opinions, every one his own way.
– Terence (c.190–159 BC)

It *can* be hard to find a psychiatrist who will fully understand us and our problems. We may need to try two or three until we've found the one who's right for us, the one we can best get along with.

If you belong to a self-help group, members might suggest doctors whom they've found helpful. Then you could ask your family doctor to refer you to that particular specialist.

The best doctor has the following strengths. He or she
- is a compassionate listener,
- does not ignore complaints about side effects, but tries to solve the problems side effects cause (if they are overly bothersome),
- stays on top of new findings in research,
- is aware of all medications available,
- is not afraid to try new medications if what the patient is taking does not work,
- is someone you can get along with.

It's important to learn all we can about our illness and the medications we're taking so that we'll be better aware of what questions to ask. This way we'll be able to work in partnership with our doctor.

Hospital Revisited

Twenty-three years had passed since my last hospitalization.
But here I was again, in 1996, needing the hospital again. I wanted it.
I truly needed some treatment to release me from a depression that had
plagued me for one and a half years. And each time I was hit by a wave of it,
I felt like I wanted to die. This death wish was new for me.
I knew I needed help. Pills alone no longer seemed to work.

Psychiatric hospitals have a reputation – a bad one. We've all seen the movies, those that paint terrifying pictures of mad patients and stern, insensitive staff. As movies generally like to do, much was exaggerated. But there was some truth to what they showed as well.

Thankfully, psychiatric wards have changed much over the years. Today there is more understanding about the illnesses. Also the new medications that are available today can help patients more than ever before. Doctors have far more options in treating us. Medical staff, with their increased understanding, treat their patients with more respect.

Today's psychiatric wards in major hospitals are good places to go when we feel depressed enough to be suicidal or manic enough to be dangerous to ourselves and others.

Here we can receive rest, protection, and care. Here we can be assessed to determine whether our medications are working effectively. In this safe, controlled environment a change in medication can be carefully administered and effects monitored.

In the hospital ward I was in, there was an ambience of friendliness amongst the staff which was picked up by the patients as well. Fellow patients were not overmedicated as they were in the past, thus a camaraderie was possible amongst us.

Doctors were frequently available to confer with, and a nurse tried whenever possible to meet any patient's request for a private talk.

Today's hospitals are good places to get well, to learn to see our life from a different perspective, and to achieve an understanding of how to improve it. A hospital gives us a place where we can temporarily escape the worries and stress of the world outside. It can provide us with a haven when we truly need it.

In hospital there's someone who will ensure that we take our medications and that we take them at the right time. We are fed nutritious foods and there are people to be with when we're lonely.

During my recent stay in hospital, I was kept active doing morning stretching exercises, swimming, and exercising in a weight room. In the afternoon I did arts and crafts. Between these activities there was ample time for resting, reading, or watching TV. There was time to spend alone on my bed, and time to mix and talk with other patients. When I was up to it, and when he was able, my husband took me home for a few hours.

I soon started to feel stronger emotionally and learned to recognize that there is hope for me. A small adjustment to my medication helped stabilize me. I also learned that there is often a difference between how things are and how I perceive them to be.

If You Can Trust Yourself...

If you can trust yourself when all men doubt you,
But make allowance for their doubting too;...
– Rudyard Kipling, *If*

If we can trust ourselves to take appropriate measures when the first symptoms of depression or mania threaten, and if we can make allowance for family's or friends' doubts and warnings when our moods cause concern, we should be able to nip our illness in the bud and overcome problems before they become severe.

When depression threatens – as we catch ourselves brooding more than we should be, getting tired by thoughts of doing the simplest chores, or showing any of the other symptoms for depression referred to earlier – it is time to talk to our doctor about possible adjustment of medications.

For those whose problem is manic depression it's essential to slow down when the threat of mania becomes apparent. We may find ourselves gradually speeding up to the point where we are faced with a huge teetering tower of projects and commitments. One day we might panic and realize that we won't be able to fulfill all our promises.

If we can see this gradual speeding up in our minds and actions, or if we will listen to the warnings of a loved one, we'll be in a position to ask others for help and to stop the manic process from taking over completely. We'll be able to stop it before it gets total control of us.

It takes a responsible person to make the decision to rely on others when they know their ability to function is temporarily impaired. We should not be ashamed of making a choice to lean on others during times of illness – in fact, it is commendable to do so.

It *is* possible to trust ourselves while recognizing that there are times when we will have to temporarily lean on others.

3

WHEN WE ARE DEPRESSED

When We Are Depressed

I realized...that every act of life from the morning toothbrush
to the friend at dinner had become an effort...
hating the night when I couldn't sleep
and hating the day because it went toward night.
– F. Scott Fitzgerald, *The Crack-up*

Yes, there *will* be times when we become depressed. In spite of the medications that help us and in spite of living a positive and active lifestyle, our mood disorders and their symptoms will probably always be a threat. What should we do at times like this, when our body feels heavy and our mind is filled with dark thoughts, when it's so hard to believe in the goodness of life?

Mood disorders are unpredictable beasts which can invade our lives when we least expect them. They often go unnoticed for weeks but gradually creep into the core of our being. One day we realize that life isn't fun anymore. We're tired all the time and nothing seems to interest us.

As we get older, it becomes somewhat easier to recognize the onset of depression. It begins with a feeling of flatness – the days have no sparkle anymore – we have little energy to do anything.

When depression takes over, we should try to remember that this *is* an illness and, like any other illness, it must run its course. In the same way as we help ourselves to feel better when we nurse a cold, we can also treat ourselves and our depression in a way that will make it more bearable.

The inability to function normally tends to make us feel frustrated, impatient, and ashamed. It is important to try to do what we comfortably can. But since this *is* an illness, we should not fight too hard but instead *go with it*, understanding that we *will* eventually get better. Patience and faith are great assets here.

When we are depressed, we tend to hide ourselves away in our room. It's worthwhile, however, to try to be around other people for at least a portion of every day. Being with others distracts us from our negative thinking and often improves our perspective. Visiting with a friend, shopping, or participating in a recreation program or club activity will help to draw us out.

Physical activity is also very effective in speeding our recovery. Walking or light exercise can help to stimulate our minds. Begin physical exercise slowly and gradually build up. As long as our exercise session is vigorous enough to make us comfortably tired at the end, our minds will benefit.

Doing things with our hands gives us another good form of therapy. This kind of activity tends to provide a feeling of vitality and of being in control. The satisfaction that comes with accomplishing something is valuable.

Simple everyday activities such as washing dishes, cooking, gardening, or working on a favorite hobby are good, even if we can only manage to work for short periods at a time.

The key is 1) to accept that you're not well and need time to recover, 2) to do what makes you feel best, and 3) not to push yourself simply because you think you should.

Your main job for yourself right now is to start feeling good again – bit by bit. Doing everything in short spurts will probably work best. Begin with only 10 or 15 minutes on an activity and alternate with rests.

A wonderful thing happens to many of us. During depression we often experience short periods when we feel somewhat better; we feel a temporary spark of energy, even if it is very small. This brightening, this "window" in our darkness, presents us with an opportunity to become active; we should not waste this opportunity. Often we'll find that these windows will gradually become wider and appear more frequently. It's very likely that, one day, we will suddenly realize that the depression is no longer with us and that life is actually quite wonderful!

Caught In a Dream World

If you can dream – and not make dreams your master;
If you can think – and not make thoughts your aim;...
– Rudyard Kipling, *If*

As part of our illness, many of us go through phases where we become lost in thought – thinking and thinking and thinking, on and on. The minutes and the hours disappear. Even the night gets eaten up by thought and we lose sleep – sleep that is so fundamental to our well-being.

This (what seems to be) perpetual daydreaming is quite pleasant at first. We savor memories and mull things over endlessly. These warm dreamy times are kind of nice. We don't really want to wake up.

However, if we don't break free from this inactivity, this seemingly innocent reverie could bear the seeds of oncoming problems. We could soon feel as though entangled in a web – not quite part of the real world.

When we decide it's time to face reality again we find ourselves caught – it's hard to move. We have become caught in the beginnings of depression. We struggle to loosen ourselves.

Sometimes at times like this Rudyard Kipling's words from his poem *If* float back to me: "If you can think – and not make thoughts your aim..." They help me escape the reverie. The world gradually becomes somewhat clearer to my eyes and mind as I begin to focus once more on actively doing things instead of just thinking about them. It's so good to see and touch the crystal of the day once more, to go outside and meet the sun, to bathe my face in its warmth, to hear the song of birds, to marvel at the tulips dazzling in their colors.

But now *I must get to work!*

A Window In the Gloom

I felt miserable – physically weak and tired – my head ached. I wasn't up to doing any of the things I normally enjoyed. Chores did not appear worth the enormous trouble they seemed to require.

Sitting in bed, I listened to the radio, once in a while nodding off. This became a bore. I tried reading, but the book didn't interest me the way it used to. Besides, the effort was more than I could comfortably manage. I lay back against the pillow, not wanting to move.

After a long while, it no longer felt good to be so lazy. I became restless and struggled in search of something useful to do, something that would remove the feeling of guilt that was building, something that would make me feel good again.

Feeling good again – I wasn't even sure I wanted that anymore. To make myself feel good would take energy I felt powerless to bring forth. The bed was warm and safe – away from the struggle of responsibilities.

But finally I did feel a little brighter and got up. I combed my hair and made my way to the kitchen. Here I puttered for 20 minutes, emptying the dishwasher. Slowly I put the clean dishes in their places in the cupboards. I filled the dishwasher with the stack of dirty dishes that had collected. Wiping the counter, I felt a little better; my mind felt more alert. I looked around the kitchen, satisfied with the improvement.

And now? But my energy wasn't up for more – nothing I wanted to do, anyway. I climbed the stairs and headed back to the bedroom, longing once more for escape to my safe nest, my secure retreat – to await the appearance of another glimmer, another window in the walls of my gloom.

A Time of Weakness*

*For the depressed can never be sure we can finish anything we begin,
or indeed certain of anything,
except the black dogs' eventual return...*
– John Bentley Mays, *In the Jaws of the Black Dogs*

Over recent years there have been numerous opportunities that I've had to pass up because I wasn't sure if I would be well enough to cope with them. I've had to turn down offers of photo assignments, speaking engagements, and requests to judge and critique photographs.

Mood disorders are unpredictable. I never know when a bout of depression or mania will take me out of commission. At times it's difficult to trust myself with almost anything.

Often the safest thing for me to do is to stick close to home, leave the answering machine on, and not make firm plans. I've always been a reliable person, yet I find I can promise less and less. Living like this lowers my self-esteem and gradually weakens my confidence.

I like to have responsibilities. I like to have an active role in my community. I need these to feel like my life is serving a useful purpose. Yet so often my moods let me down and I have to disappoint those I was working with.

As the years progress this seems to cause more and more problems. It's as though my ability to keep my life balanced is deteriorating with each passing year, especially lately. Where is the joy I used to know? It surfaces now and then, but does so less and less.

I fight to survive and remain a part of this world, yet find myself slowly slipping away.

Author's note: Written during one and a half years of depression following the initial draft of Riding the Roller Coaster. *A year later, on a new and more effective medication, these feelings had completely disappeared. I felt happy and confident, once more working on a wide variety of projects.*

When Life Doesn't Seem Worth Living

I have never tried to take my life, although I have often wished I could die.
Sometimes life really does seem unbearable. At times like this
I have difficulty believing there's a way out of the blackness
that seems to envelop me. But, invariably, things do improve –
the days do become filled with color again.
I know of individuals who have taken their own lives.
They couldn't see their way out of the misery.

The trouble is that these people could not think beyond themselves. They forgot that there were friends and family members who loved them. If they had only realized what their death would mean to these people. If they had only known how much they would be missed, and what a hole they would leave in the lives of their loved ones. Often those who are left behind blame themselves, wondering what they did wrong. They wonder what they could have done to avoid the tragedy. They suffer greatly.

Most of the people close to you care a lot more about you than they ever say. It's difficult for most of us to express our love fully to our friends. But that doesn't mean that the love isn't there.

When you feel so bad that life doesn't seem worth living anymore, try talking to someone close to you. Try to express clearly how you feel. Listen carefully to what your friend has to say to you. Although they may find it difficult to say in so many words that they love you, you may very well sense it in their concern. Try not to keep all those bad thoughts locked inside. It helps to get them into the open – to let others know – to get help.

With a friend or family member's help, see your family doctor or psychiatrist or go to the emergency department of a psychiatric hospital or general hospital for help. If you are admitted as a patient, the hospital will provide a safe and therapeutic environment. Doctors can assess your progress as they adjust your medications and find which is best for you.

Depression *is* treatable. Don't give up.

If I Cry Out Please Listen

When I'm feeling deeply dark and don't know where there's an out for me – when I've forgotten God is there – when I feel utter shame and see no way to fix the wrongs I've done, I search for a place for my river to flow.

But friends have come to think me a crying pest. I can feel it so strongly. They try to treat me as a counselor should, in a businesslike fashion. I don't blame them; they have worries of their own.

I reach out to those I consider close, but soon feel shame. When can I go to them in joy again? Why always the tears? And why don't they reach out to me once in a while?

If only friends could understand that when I cry out to them, it's because I feel they may be my last resort. It's because I thought they might help me find some light. I wouldn't bother them so much if I were well. It's not out of boredom that I call.

But when the blackness overcomes me, all that I can do when I hit that wall is cry for help. It's impossible to live this life if there's nowhere for my river to flow.

Escaping the Blues Before They Grab Me

When Christmas draws near I, along with millions of others, get in step with the festivities and all the work that entails: baking, decorating, shopping for gifts and wrapping them, going to parties, sending cards and letters. Altogether, about one and a half months are taken up by these unusually busy times. It seems as though everything I do during this period is aimed at getting ready for that one day. In fact, I almost feel guilty when I do anything that is not connected to the festivities.

I began to see that, when January came, I would experience a letdown – a letdown that in years past was difficult to boost myself out of. Suddenly, life became normal again – and colorless: the tree was gone, the glitter of decorations had disappeared. Everything had turned flat. There seemed to be no clear purpose to the days anymore.

That's how it used to be. But several years ago I learned that if I planned a "meaty" project to begin the new year with, there was no post-Christmas letdown. There was only the anticipation of having the time for a new creative adventure. And this provided a color of its own.

Since learning this approach to the new year, much of my most creative work has been done in the months following Christmas. It was simply the result of a plan to escape the blues – a way to get my mood under control before it got me under its control.

Things to do When You Don't Feel Like Doing Anything

Below is a list for times when you feel so down that absolutely nothing seems worth the effort. Some of these suggestions may seem rather nonsensical, but if you can muster up the energy to do one or two of them when you're depressed, you may be on your way to recovery. Are you game to try?

- Change the scenery – move to a different room.
- Take a sip of soda – let the bubbles dance on your tongue.
- Wash your face and comb your hair – that feels *so* good!
- Listen to gentle music – become a part of it.
- Eat a piece of sweet juicy fruit.
- Hug your pillow – pretend it's your best friend.
- Pick a flower from the garden – study its shape, color and texture – smell its perfume.
- Take a refreshing shower – *Enjoy*.
- Bask in the sunshine – 10 minutes will do the trick – or,

- Point your face to the sky – let the rain wash your cheeks.
- Write a description of your feelings – get poetic if you wish.
- Watch a comedy on TV – the sillier, the better.
- Blow bubbles in the bathtub.
- Make a list of everything you're thankful for.
- Beg a hug from someone close to you – squeeze hard.
- Lie under a tree – look into its branches – listen to the whisper of the leaves.
- Have a cup of tea with a friend.

Things to do When You Can Cope a Little

When we begin to sense a little pleasure again, we need to encourage these feelings by being good to ourselves. We should concentrate on activities that will make us feel good – activities that we do, not because we *should* do them, but because we *want* to.

- Write in a journal.
- Tidy up a small area of your home.
- Go for a walk.
- Buy a gift or card for a friend.
- Have a bath with a deluxe bar of soap.
- Cook a simple meal.
- Buy yourself a "sinful" treat.
- Phone a friend.
- Listen to your favorite music.
- Get your hair done.
- Putter at a hobby.

Things to do When You Feel Stronger

Many of the following activities are organizational in nature. When we're moderately depressed, these activities will take our mind off the negative thinking that is so hard to shake. They are also good therapy for times when we are a bit high and need to slow down. The activity will help us regain a sense of control. It's satisfying to complete jobs that we had meant to do for a long time.

In the company of your favorite music:
- Organize your recipes.
- Work on a hobby.
- Tidy the workshop.
- Plant something in the garden.
- Tidy a messy room.
- Catch up on the ironing.
- Go for a walk.
- Wash the car.
- Cook a special meal with a friend.
- Organize your photo collection in albums.
- Do a jigsaw puzzle.
- Phone or get together with a friend who's down.

Anxiety

I am still so timid and fearful that I cannot sleep alone...
Do you believe that I have not the courage to travel alone...
for fear something might befall me?
– Robert Schumann, F. Niecks' *Robert Schumann*

When we're depressed and our ability to function normally is decreased, it's only natural that our accompanying loss of confidence can lead to an overall anxiety. We become anxious about such simple things as going out-of-doors, crossing the street, getting lost.

Some of us become so anxious that, once in a while, it even becomes difficult to eat a meal. We tremble, overcome with uncertainty. Our forks and knives become difficult to manage. The food is dry or we take bites that are too big. We almost choke.

Anxiety is a fear that grips us and seems as though it won't let us go – we have lost faith in our ability to do even the simplest thing.

Anxiety is the root of paranoia, the condition some of us have when we don't trust people or when we feel we're being plotted against.

In others, it's also responsible for the onset of panic attacks – those sudden, unexpected surges of feeling breathless – as though we're about to die.

It is when we try to work on small tasks such as washing the dishes or tidying a room that we will begin to feel better. It's when we muster the will to do the little things that we'll be on the road to completing the bigger jobs and the more creative projects. And with these will come the feeling of accomplishment and satisfaction.

4

WHEN WE ARE MANIC

With Feet Firmly On the Ground

You can have no greater friend than your mind if it is under your control.
And you can have no greater enemy than your mind
if it is not under your control.
– Author Unknown

Many of us who have a bipolar mood disorder may have experienced our first manic episode in our late teens or early 20s. Our mood gradually became elevated. We didn't realize what was happening to us; the feelings were new and foreign. The idea that we had a mental illness was the farthest thing from our minds. Our mood, unbridled, became expansive; we felt we could do anything. Sometimes we became psychotic, experiencing delusions of grandeur, a feeling that we were extraordinary; some of us may even have believed ourselves to be a religious figure with great powers.

When we have our initial episodes of mania, we often welcome this perception of ourselves. We're young, self-esteem is often low, and the grandiose feelings make us see ourselves as something special. We don't discourage our lofty thought patterns at all, but revel in the dream world they present to us.

As we grow older, however, and experience more crises, we learn to recognize the early symptoms when they arise. We learn to listen when someone close to us warns us of the danger we're in. If our life is well-balanced and we understand our illness sufficiently, we get to know when it is time to go to the doctor for help. As we become older and wiser, and if we have a healthy self-esteem, we come to value the world of reality above all else. We no longer want the loss of control. It's great being part of a community and being able to relate to the people in it and have them relate to us. We learn that there is nothing as fantastic as having our two feet firmly planted on the ground...and we work hard to keep them there.

Overstimulation

...sometimes I am so full of music, and so overflowing with melody,
that I find it simply impossible to write down anything.
– Robert Schumann, J. Hermand and J. Steakley's,
Writings of German Composers

Those of us with manic depression sometimes have times when the world around us seems extremely delightful, intensely fascinating. The simple act of shopping in the local mall can give us too many things to look at; we are oversensitive to stimuli. Our mind wants to absorb and interpret every colorful detail: the shoppers, young and old, so interesting to watch; the goods for sale, beautiful dresses, attractive shirts. Everywhere we look there is color and activity. We soon become overwhelmed. "Our cup runneth over."

This tends to happen especially at times when our mood is elevated. Our minds move faster than normal and we are unusually alert to everything happening around us. We gradually find ourselves overstimulated. This is one of the danger signs which indicates we could be heading for a severe manic episode.

If we can learn to see this happening to us, we may be able to prevent ourselves from getting sick by seeing our doctor and having our medications adjusted temporarily.

While we wait for the medications to take effect, it's important to try to simplify our life, to stay away from anything that is too interesting or exciting to us. This may be a good time to focus on something basic, such as working on a simple hobby or organizing the household – maybe not easy things to do at a time like this, but it *will* help us to slow down.

When we've lived with our illness for several years, it becomes remarkable how we can learn to recognize symptoms before they get out of hand. By understanding ourselves, we can often avoid serious problems.

Rudyard Kipling's Gift

Lying on the hospital bed in the emergency room, I felt agitated and filled the time yelling insults at the nurses and doctors. The quiet young girl I normally was had turned wild. Nothing made sense anymore. I felt like a trapped monster with reason and emotion out of control. Before leaving home I'd had enough sense to grab something of my own, something precious to me, to take along. Somehow I had felt that I would be going somewhere for quite a while so I brought along an anthology of poems as company, an old textbook from high school.

After what seemed like a very long time, a doctor came to talk to me. He asked me questions about what I was feeling. His manner was kind. He seemed to understand what I was going through. Finally he picked up my book and, after browsing through it for a minute, found a poem and asked me to read it out loud. The poem was a well-known one, although not to me at the time. I slowly started to read *If* by Rudyard Kipling, struggling to bring my head into focus:

> If you can keep your head when all about you
> Are losing theirs and blaming it on you;
> If you can trust yourself when all men doubt you,
> But make allowance for their doubting too;

As I read, my brain cleared somewhat. The message was strong and it registered well. I felt as though this had been written for people with problems very much like mine. I could see that this poet knew what it was to struggle and how to overcome severe difficulty. I felt that I was not alone.

By the time I had finished reading the poem I had become subdued and, even though I was very sick, I had found a source of inspiration. I had found something that would help me tackle life anew. My eyes closed and I fell asleep – at peace.

I've often wished I knew who the doctor was who introduced me to this poem. I wish I could thank him and tell him how much he helped me. And if Rudyard Kipling had only known how much his writing could mean to someone!

Ever since that night, his poem has been very special to me. I carried it with me for years. Even now, lines from it often float back to me reminding me how to live, inspiring me to believe in myself and be strong.

If

If you can keep your head when all about you
Are losing theirs and blaming it on you;
If you can trust yourself when all men doubt you,
But make allowance for their doubting too;
If you can wait and not be tired by waiting,
Or, being lied about, don't deal in lies,
Or, being hated, don't give way to hating,
And yet don't look too good, nor talk too wise;
If you can dream – and not make dreams your master;
If you can think – and not make thoughts your aim;
If you can meet with Triumph and Disaster
And treat those two impostors just the same;
If you can bear to hear the truth you've spoken
Twisted by knaves to make a trap for fools,
Or watch the things you gave your life to broken,
And stoop and build 'em up with worn-out tools;

If you can make one heap of all your winnings
And risk it on one turn of pitch-and-toss,
And lose, and start again at your beginnings
And never breathe a word about your loss;
If you can force your heart and nerve and sinew
To serve your turn long after they are gone,
And so hold on when there is nothing in you
Except the Will which says to them: "Hold on";
If you can talk with crowds and keep your virtue,
Or walk with Kings – nor lose the common touch;
If neither foes nor loving friends can hurt you;
If all men count with you, but none too much;
If you can fill the unforgiving minute
With sixty seconds' worth of distance run –
Yours is the Earth and everything that's in it,
And – which is more – you'll be a Man, my son!

– Rudyard Kipling

A Time to Dance

I don't get manic as often as I used to, thanks to my medications. But once in a while I still get somewhat so, especially when my creative projects are coming along well. Satisfaction with my work turns my mood into one of exhilaration.

At times I feel a bit like Mr. Scrooge in the last scenes of Dickens' *A Christmas Carol*. After the last ghost, the Spirit of Christmas Future, leaves him and he wakes up to reality, he realizes that he still has time to live the way he should have lived all along.

Much like Scrooge, I feel joyous, at times even dancing around the living room to express myself. I'm exuberant, inspired – my energy becomes seemingly boundless.

On days like this there is so much I want to do and say – my mind floods with ideas. I volunteer for one job after another, not realizing that I'm overextending myself. I love everyone and let many of them know it too – making phone calls to friends, some of whom I haven't spoken to for a long time. I have conversations that might, at times of better balance, embarrass me. The world looks like a wonderful place and, with my camera, I explore the parks, trying to make weeds look as beautiful as plants in a garden (though that's not as crazy as you may think).

I go to bed late, not wanting to put an end to my day, my mind too active for sleep.

After Mania

*I feel such embarrassment, even shame, for some of the things I've done because of this crazy illness! In the morning I awake and remember –
and it becomes hard to get up and face the day.
I thank God for my dear kitten who comes to lick my hand –
encouraging me, reminding me that this is a new day.
I don't have to dwell on the old.*

Probably the saddest and most serious consequences of our disorder (especially the mania) are financial and legal problems, and the damage we can do to relationships.

Some of us overspend drastically; some give to others more than they can afford; some make promises they could never keep. We embarrass ourselves in public, doing or saying things that others consider strange, thus damaging our reputation. Although we may feel happy, excited and full of life within, on the outside, to others, we appear to be acting unnaturally, to be out of control.

Remember that many of the mistakes we make are due to our illness. Our disorder causes us to do many things we otherwise would not do. When the manic episode wears off, we are left with feelings of guilt, shame, and self-hatred. Looking back to see what we've done often causes such pain that we drop into a deep depression. It's possible to shorten this fall by taking responsibility for our mistakes, by going back to correct them.

It's wrong to think that because the "dumb" things we did were the result of our mood disorder, they are okay. We are still responsible and we must do whatever we can – as humiliating as it may feel – to rectify our wrongs. Facing our mistakes in this way will show others that we're doing our best. It will boost our damaged self-esteem.

Treat each manic episode as a learning experience, planning what to do to avoid similar problems in the future: for example, keep less cash on hand and learn to respect our family's and friends' warnings when they recognize we're in trouble.

These are the tough realities of bipolar disorder. We have to face these challenges in order to live with our illness. If we can do this courageously there will be opportunities for a satisfying and productive life.

When My Judgment Is Off

One of the most painful elements of my illness is when I'm unstable and my sense of judgment becomes poor in the things I do, say, and write. I am so aware of how this can happen and yet I do it over and over – and this makes me feel terrible so much of the time.

I've learned to rely on the judgment of my husband, Wes, and to ask him to read what I've written and get his opinion of how I should handle situations on the phone. And yet, while he's at work and I'm left with the telephone and fax machine, I can sure pull some "doozies." Thankfully, with Wes's counseling, I've managed to keep most of my friends.

Most people have problems because they tend to procrastinate. My problem is the reverse – I usually feel that everything has to be done immediately. In my mind, when I make a decision to talk to someone or to begin some kind of work, I feel the need to do that right away, without giving it adequate thought. Even when I'm convinced that it's okay it often turns out to be a very stupid thing to do – and am I sorry later! My confidence takes a real beating!

Self-esteem

It is not what he has, nor even what he does,
which directly affects the worth of a man; but what he is.
– Henri-Frédéric Amiel

When we have a major episode of depression, mania, or psychosis we often come out of it with low self-esteem. The stormy psychological battles that we experience can cause us to feel as though we've become useless and don't have any value. Some of us lose a job or friends or even a wife or husband due to our illness. Hospital experiences tend to be demoralizing as well.

There is also much difficult coping: not just with the symptoms, but also with the idea of having the illness in the first place. Sometimes we tend to believe, along with society, that our disorder reflects our personality. We should remember that such ideas result from the stigma society has wrongfully attached to mental illness. *There is no relationship between our illness and our self-worth.*

As our moods change, our self-image changes. When we feel down, we tend to look at ourselves in a very negative way – we think we're failures. When we are manic, our opinion of ourselves becomes inflated – we think we're wonderful, even superhuman. Both of these extreme feelings are unreasonable. The truth of the matter is that both the extreme negative and the extreme positive attitudes are irrational. We are really somewhere in between. Our true worthiness does not change at all; we are worth as much as every other person. Only our view of ourselves changes, colored by what our mood is at the time.

When we mutter negative comments to ourselves within the privacy of our thoughts, it's important to realize that we are not being rational.

Labeling ourselves or generalizing about what we feel are our shortcomings is very damaging and can cause further depression. This kind of internal dialogue keeps us from moving ahead with the positive attitude we all need to be happy and confident. We should not allow these thoughts to continue unchallenged. Rather, we should stifle them by talking back, working toward a more positive point of view. Much can be done by carrying on *positive* internal dialogues with ourselves.

What we are is not determined by what others think of us or by what we achieve. Everyone has an equal worthiness and there is no such thing as a worthless person. We will be content when we believe this and accept and love ourselves for who we are.

Attitudes to Build Self-esteem

The following list of positive attitudes or affirmations can help us if we read it and take it to heart when we have a hard time feeling good about ourselves.

- I can be happy, even if I'm not accepted by all people at all times.
- If I make a mistake, it does not mean I'm inept.
- Although I'll miss you, I can live without you.
- Just because somebody disagrees with me doesn't mean that person doesn't like me.
- What others think of me has no bearing on my value as a person.
- It's okay to be embarrassed once in a while.
- If I lose control of my emotions now and then, it does not mean that I'll go crazy.
- Showing my inner weaknesses to others once in a while is not such a bad thing.

Reunion

Friends of my parents gathered, a crowded roomful of faces, many of them familiar ones I had almost forgotten. It takes a big occasion like this 50th wedding anniversary to bring together individuals such as these, so many of them carrying memories of me from my younger years.

As they say hello I wonder what they think of me. These "friends of the family" knew me when I was growing up and still living at home. They knew me when I became ill and spent months in an institution. What are their thoughts of me now?

They've missed my years of wellness. They've missed my years of ability. They don't know me as the whole person I've become. Do they still think of me as strange?

They shake my hand and ask how I am, but don't really wait for a reply. They treat me as though I'm a stranger – someone they're not sure how to talk to. The brief meeting passes and they move on.

The pain of being thought of as "that person who had such bad problems" is forever present. So many people, many of whom meant a lot to me, have not known me in these later years. They don't realize that I've risen above my problems. To them, am I still a strange one?

Sometimes I wish I could take a few weeks and spend time with each estranged friend from the past, people I worked with and went to school with, so that we could get to know each other again. I wish I had a chance to let them know I'm okay and that I've grown up to be not unlike them. I want to be considered normal. I wish people could look at me, forgetting about my history. I want to be just me again.

5

KEEPING LIFE STABLE

Keeping Life Stable

When mania hits or depression strikes,
don't take the shingles from the roof of your comfort
to light a fire for the warmth of a moment.
– Robert Winram, Mood Disorder Association of B.C.

When we become depressed or manic, the natural tendency is to give up the rules for healthy living that we know are good for us. All too easily we give up our routines, choosing instead to do whatever feels good at the moment. We might drink too much; we might forget the importance of adequate sleep and stay up all night; we often forget mealtimes.

To guard against this, it is important to build a lifestyle that can form a strong, stable canopy over our day-to-day life – a roof, protecting us from the storms that mood swings bring. This lifestyle would keep us steady while we are well and help us get back on our feet when we are not. We would not be as easily tempted to destroy it.

A stable life is a well-balanced one. If our life were like this to begin with, it would be easier to abide by routine, easier to remain disciplined when we experience the ups and downs. Regular mealtimes, bedtimes, and "getting up" times are important to a stable way of life. Filling each day with some social interaction and some solitude, some work and some play, some giving and some receiving (you get the idea), in accordance with our individual needs, will provide us with balance. This will go far to protect us from attacks of depression and mania.

When sickness *does* come, there will also then be less temptation to change our life severely. The rules we live by, the tools for maintaining our health, will be so ingrained that it will be easier to keep them functioning. It's less likely that our way of life will crumble – more likely that we will recover quickly.

A balanced, stable life is one that is strong enough to withstand slight mood swings and to fight the severe ones. Mood disorders are not just problems we forget about until they come along and need to be "fixed"; our day-to-day living needs to fight the possible onset of highs and lows on a continuous basis.

Motherhood

My life became much more stable soon after my son was born. Once I had overcome the shock and accompanying mood problems, I settled down into the routine having a baby requires: feeding times, rest times, bath times, and so forth.

I ate and went to bed on a set schedule – no chance to laze about the way I used to. To be the good mother I wanted to be, I had to adhere to my schedule of chores: washing and folding diapers, mixing formula, sterilizing bottles, as well as all the work of keeping house that I did before.

With my new lifestyle as a mother, I found I became healthier mentally. I didn't have as many problems with my mood swings as I used to have.

Was my more disciplined lifestyle the reason for my better health? Or was my new responsibility and the special need to be well partly the reason for my new coping ability? Does motherhood naturally bring a strength with it – a strength to fulfill the role I had been given?

Or was it simply that I had this beautiful new life to love and care for?

Managing Stress

Why really, the land spins around as does a potter's wheel.
– Ipuwer, Ancient Egyptian Prophet (c.2200 BC)

Stress is the physical or emotional factor that causes us to feel tension in our bodies and minds. It is known to have a big effect on our health. Most stress occurs as a result of changes – and our lives are full of changes. It's impossible to avoid them. If we are to stay well we need to learn how to live successfully with these fluctuations in our lives.

Some pressures are a healthy thing. Change, and the stress that comes with it, makes life spicy, colorful, exciting. But if more change is demanded than we can comfortably cope with and the stress becomes too great, then we could end up sick. Illnesses made worse by excessive stress span almost the entire range of medical problems: tuberculosis, diabetes, the common cold, athletic injuries, as well as depression and anxiety. The same kind of stress that contributes to a heart attack in one person, can, in another person, trigger a psychotic episode.

Excessive stress touches everyone's life now and then. The death of a spouse, divorce, personal injury, marriage, retirement, pregnancy, a new job, a change in sleeping and eating habits, and even a vacation – all of these things create significant amounts of stress. Notice that it's not only the negative changes that cause us problems; positive changes can also lead to illness.

We who have a susceptibility to illness need to make sure that we structure our lives so that the effects of stress will be minimized. Pacing ourselves by trying not to plan too many big changes all at once will help. If we know that a potentially stressful event is coming up it would be wise to plan it well. When we're well prepared for a situation we'll be able to handle it with confidence and with a relaxed state of mind.

Being well organized when it comes to managing our activities and our environment will help us feel in control and thus, less stressed. It's hard to feel relaxed when we're unsure whether we're meeting our responsibilities or not, when we've lost track of important papers, or when we've forgotten to buy milk for tomorrow's cereal. Keeping lists is a great way to reduce this kind of stress significantly. All busy people rely on lists of things to do, appointments to keep, and groceries to buy.

Harboring intense feelings can also cause much stress. This is why it's healthy to give vent to our feelings by talking about them with a friend or therapist, by expressing them in art work, by singing or dancing, or by writing in a journal. Keeping emotions locked up inside can make us feel a bit like a volcano, ready to burst. It's better to allow the steam to escape little by little; this will cause far less damage.

Physical Exercise

A feeble body weakens the mind.
– Jean Jacques Rousseau, *Émile*

Physical exercise provides a major way of coping with mental stress. It is believed that, for milder cases of depression, exercise is as effective as psychotherapy. Regular exercise also helps us maintain a positive outlook on life.

We should choose the forms of physical exercise we can enjoy or learn to enjoy doing. Many people make their exercise time a social event. By getting together with others to jog, hike or swim, we will have the support and encouragement we need. We'll be more likely to carry on with the program and we'll have more fun.

Work around the house: cleaning, painting, remodeling, or gardening. Have a picnic with friends, complete with kite flying, volleyball and a swim in the lake. Or enjoy music and socializing as you go dancing on a Saturday night. We can exercise our bodies while we work or play. We'll feel invigorated and, at the same time, achieve a relaxed mental state.

Some of the numerous exercise options include jogging, walking, cycling, roller blading, playing raquet sports, canoeing, and backpacking. The important thing is to get our bodies moving as they were meant to move.

Today, almost everyone is aware of the importance physical fitness plays in our health. Almost all of us have opportunities to take exercise classes on a regular basis. Public recreation centers as well as private fitness centers offer a great assortment of classes, something to suit everyone. There are mild, moderate, and intense workouts; pool workouts and gym workouts; workouts for seniors and new mothers; skating and weight training. Almost every community offers some of these.

Relaxation

May the outward and the inward man be as one.
– Socrates (469–399 BC)

It's rather difficult for an anxious mind to live in a relaxed body. By relaxing our body we will remove tension in our mind and bring a calmness to our entire being. If we can teach our bodies to release tension fully when we are under stress, we will be able to bring the stress under control.

A number of different relaxation techniques can help us when we are tense. Some of these involve deep breathing. With practice we can learn to use these kinds of relaxation responses each time we feel tense. We learn to recognize when we are stressed and to use the breathing technique to return our body to a relaxed state. This response can be used anywhere: in a supermarket lineup, as we go into an important job interview, or as our plane is taking off. (Two brief relaxation techniques follow this essay.)

Periodic rest breaks during each day will help to relax our body and mind and result in better ability to cope with pressures. Sitting occasionally in a favorite chair with a book or some music can provide effective rest. Many of us find that spending 10 or 15 minutes in quiet prayer or meditation will revive us. Naps are valuable, but best if they're kept short so that they don't interfere with our sleep at night.

A humor break should be part of everyone's regular weekly plan. Watching a comedy from the video store, reading a book of jokes and passing them along, or playing lighthearted games with our friends can do wonders to remove the tenseness in our muscles. Laughing gives us an emotional release we all need from time to time. It's healing and helps us to see the bright side of things.

Often our lives tend to become so full of events, activities, and work that we feel as though we're on a merry-go-round that won't stop. We'd desperately like to get off, but it's so hard. This indicates that we need time out, time to stop running, time to get things into perspective. If a true holiday is out of the question, a mini-holiday in the form of a dinner out, or an evening at the theater can help to remove us for a while from our busy life. A drive in the country, a hike in the mountains, or a picnic at a local park can be the break we need to relieve stress.

Relaxation Techniques

These two brief relaxation techniques are simple to learn and can be done when your body feels tense or when you want to let go of a worry.

Practice them 10 to 15 times a day for several weeks. Try to remember to use them at transition times during the day. For example, in the car while waiting for a light to turn green, when moving from one activity to another, or in the supermarket in the checkout line.

The first technique, called the "Calming Breath," takes about 20 seconds to do. It can be used when you want a quick and easy way to begin relaxing.

To release the tension in your muscles, before or after this breath, you may want to literally shake your hands and arms and each of your legs for a few seconds. While doing this, imagine you are shaking free from all those worried, uptight thoughts and loosening the tension from your muscles.

Calming Breath

1. Take a long, slow breath in through your nose, first filling your lower lungs, then your upper lungs.
2. Hold your breath to the count of three.
3. Exhale slowly through pursed lips while you relax the muscles in your face, jaw, shoulders, and stomach.

The second brief relaxation technique is called "Calming Counts." It requires only slightly more than a minute's time. It provides you with a longer opportunity to quiet your mind and body. It's also a good way to stop repetitious, unproductive thinking. This exercise should be done in a quiet place without interruption.

Calming Counts

1. Take a long, deep breath and exhale it slowly while saying the word "relax" silently.
2. Close your eyes and imagine your body beginning to relax.
3. Let yourself take ten gentle, easy breaths. Count down, inhale and exhale, saying "ten" on the exhalation. Next, inhale and exhale, saying "nine." Continue doing this, noticing any tensions, perhaps in your jaw, forehead, or stomach. Imagine those tensions loosening.
4. When you reach "one," open your eyes again.

Power Naps

I'm one of those lucky ones who's able to put their head down, sleep for 10 or 15 minutes, and awake, thoroughly rested and refreshed.

These power naps are important to me. I don't take them every day, but when I do, my batteries become fully recharged – I have a new lease on the day.

These naps have been part of my life since my early 20s. During the years when I worked, I daily cradled my head in my arms on the lunchroom table and allowed myself to drift off for a few minutes. When I awoke, the tired, stressed-out feeling was gone and I had energy to carry on.

Nutritious Eating

One cannot think well, love well, sleep well,
if one has not dined well.
– Virginia Woolf, *A Room of One's Own*

If we're to have a healthy mind, we also need a healthy body. It's common knowledge that the two work together. Eating a wide variety of foods is a good way to make sure we're getting all the nutrients our body requires.

Whole and enriched grain products form the basis for most of our diets. Bread, cereals, pasta, and rice are some of the major foods in this category. We should eat three to five servings per day.

Vegetables and fruits are also very important. We should try to eat four or five servings a day, including at least two kinds of green and orange vegetables, as well as different kinds of fruits.

Some of the dairy products to include in our diet are two servings of milk, cheese, or yogurt a day. The ones with lower fat content are the healthiest.

The meat we eat should be lean as often as possible. Fish provides a healthy source of protein, as does chicken, especially if we remove the skin before cooking. Alternatives to meat products are eggs, beans, and nuts. We should eat two servings per day.

Three balanced meals per day with foods selected from each of the four above categories will keep us well fed. Having fixed mealtimes is a good habit to get into. Setting time aside to relax and eat will slow us down when we're overly busy and give us something positive to focus on when we're on the low side. Sharing our meals with others makes this time especially valuable – a time to touch base with others in the household.

Comfort Foods

There are two major types of food that we choose to comfort us when we're feeling depressed or insecure.

The commonly termed "junk foods" form one category of comfort food. These include such things as chocolate bars, potato and taco chips, pretzels, donuts, and buttered popcorn. These are the foods we tend to attack in a nervous frenzy, consuming them greedily, as if there were no tomorrow. They taste good, fill an emotional and physical hunger, but are not really healthy for us.

The other category of comfort food is more often than not the kind of food we were brought up with. These are usually nourishing and remind us of our childhood – a time when we were being looked after by someone who loved us. They feed more than just a physical hunger. They can help comfort us when we are not stable and feel insecure.

It's not surprising that often these foods include milk, the first sustenance we knew as babies, as a major ingredient. Some common comfort foods are warm milk, porridge, rice pudding with raisins, macaroni and cheese, mashed potatoes with gravy, grilled cheese sandwiches, ice cream, chicken noodle soup, scrambled eggs on toast, pea soup, hot chocolate, and bananas.

Having our favorite comfort foods (especially the nutritious kind) when we're feeling out of sorts is one way to be good to ourselves. We will receive a feeling of calmness and well-being.

Stir-fry

I chop and slice the vegetables. Morsels of different shapes and textures make up my collection which I deposit in a shallow bowl. There are the greens of celery, broccoli, and snow peas, and the bright orange of sliced carrots. The frying pan sizzles as I squeeze a clove of garlic through my press into the hot peanut oil. The warm familiar aroma fills the kitchen. I add the veggies and stir slowly. The colors brighten as the vegetables fry. Minutes later I toss in some toasted almonds. I feel happy – very creative – alive. Something wholesome is taking shape in my frying pan. Now I add a sauce, including one of my favorite flavorings, ginger. Toss and heat through and *voila!* I add a pot of steamed rice and have a delicious dinner for myself and my family.

I have always loved to cook. But there are times when I'm not well enough to function normally. Performing my normal duties around the house becomes very difficult. Nevertheless I almost always carry on with my cooking, although the dinners I make at times like these often become very simple – even minimal.

When I become psychotic or manic, I find it hard to concentrate. It becomes difficult to be organized. These are the times I need to do some cooking. There's nothing like baking a cake to make me slow down so that I can follow the instructions one line at a time. At times like this that's not an easy thing to do. Once it took me two hours to bake a simple cake, but in the end, I was satisfied that I had something to serve and that I had done something productive.

Good food has color, is attractive and tasty. It appeals to all our senses. Food fills more than just my physical hunger. It is a source of joy; cooking it is a source of satisfaction.

Handling Our Finances

A budget is a method of worrying before you spend
instead of afterwards.
– Author Unknown

Handling finances can, at times, be difficult for those with mood disorders. When we are manic or depressed, concentration on our affairs can become a problem. We become forgetful, overlook paying bills, and we lose track of what we have (and don't have) in the bank.

Those of us who suffer from mania often overspend – to a very large degree. If you know this to be one of your characteristics, make a decision to live without credit cards. This will make it more difficult to spend, and greatly minimize the potential for losses.

For most of us there is a limit to the amount of disposable cash we have to spend on living expenses between paycheques. Sometimes we find that, before we realize it, we've overspent on clothing and recreation and not left enough money for the groceries. A solution to this could be to separate our available cash into envelopes for items like groceries, gas or bus fare, clothing, recreation, and miscellaneous. Then, when we go out to a movie or shop for a new pair of shoes, if we leave the grocery money safely at home we can rest assured that we'll be eating the next day. This kind of budgeting allows us to keep a tight rein on our money and helps us to make it last to the next payday.

In this modern day, we have many options to simplify our financial lives. We can have our paycheques automatically deposited to our bank account. We can also have some of our bills paid by preauthorized withdrawal. Utility bills can often be paid on an equal payment plan, a great way to avoid the "big bill" surprises in the winter. Rent could be paid by a series of postdated cheques several months at a time (just make sure there's money in the bank to cover them). These management techniques are a true godsend for when we are sick and, as so often happens, out of touch with our day-to-day obligations.

Being organized about financial responsibilities is important in everyone's life. For those of us with mood disorders, it's especially so. But the feeling that comes from doing it well is a very positive one. It is good to be in control.

Quiet Times

The peace of the contemplative is at once the most beautiful
and the most fruitful acts of man.
– Stephen Mackenna, *Journals and Letters*

Often the world seems to be just too much a part of our lives. We work and play, surrounded by people and machines. Our time is blocked out with busy schedules. We forget what it is to be by ourselves, away from all the bustle. Even when we finally get through the day, many of us turn on the radio or TV for more noise, more busyness with which to fill our heads. Many of us forget how to enjoy the peace of solitude. In fact, in this modern world, we often seem to fear it.

I believe that there is great value in reserving periods in the day for quietness: time for reflection, prayer, reading, or writing. We all need a chance to get away from the world, to get in touch with what is inside our innermost being. It's important to stop running once in a while, to pause and touch the moment.

The first part of the morning is a good time to devote to ourselves, preferably before other members of the household are up. In this silent hour, before the world has had a chance to grab us, we can plan, perhaps do some reading, and get mentally prepared for what we want to bring to our day.

The evening presents a good opportunity as well for many of us. It's at this time that we need to unwind and relax. This is a good chance to absorb the day's events and get prepared for the night's sleep. It's a chance to adjust attitudes, to boost the spirits when we're feeling low and to level out when we're high.

It's good, once in a while, to empty our mind of everything that is connected to matters of the world and fill it instead with those thoughts and ideas that matter to us personally. This is a time to dream, a time to bring our life into perspective, a time to choose tomorrow's path.

This is the hour to gather fuel for the courage we will need when we step out into the world again. It is the hour to work out what it is we value and what we want to work for. Through reading, writing, reflection, and prayer we can (inside our heads) create patterns for living that could become manifested in our world outside.

To take time to be alone and peacefully come to terms with our inner selves – to step back and gain perspective on what our life is and what we would like it to be – means that we will have ample opportunity to take control of our days and make them what we would like them to be. Quiet reflection every day can relieve the stress of modern living and help us to lead a more complete and satisfying life.

Withdrawal

I often feel the need to withdraw – whether I'm up or down. Whenever I've spent time with groups of people or when I've been busy with work, I usually feel the need to go to my bedroom to "get myself together again." I need time to be by myself – to rest and reflect.

I believe that these times of withdrawal must be my way of coping with stress. After a few minutes or half an hour on my own like this, I feel refreshed – ready to carry on.

Sitting on my bed with my back resting against a propped-up pillow is my favorite place to be. This is where I make phone calls, listen to the radio, read or write, and review plans. My most prized books are here, my desk and computer, my filing cabinet, and pictures of some of my favorite people.

This is my little corner of quiet seclusion – my comfort in a fast and oft confusing world.

Sleeplessness

To all, to each, a fair good-night,
and pleasing dreams, and slumbers light.
– Sir Walter Scott, *Marmion*

Insomnia is common with many people. For those with depression and manic depression, however, the difficulty can be especially serious. Sleep disorders are symptoms of both mania and depression.

Late at night, when the whole world seems to have come to a stop, feelings of loneliness, fear, and despair are intensified. It's easy to feel isolated and to get carried away with worries and irrational thinking. It's difficult to relax enough to allow ourselves to drop off to sleep. After several restless and sleepless nights like this we tend to dread going to bed; our attitude is fearful and negative and we're frequently beaten before we even try.

Sleeping pills can be an answer when we have lost a large amount of sleep and when our functioning is severely affected. But they are a dangerous alternative – something we should not make a habit of. Most sleeping pills are addictive and we could soon find ourselves relying on them.

It is very helpful to have a fixed routine for bedtime, one to which we adhere every night. It's also important to allow for a period of unwinding at the same time each evening before we go to bed. This could include quiet activities like reading, watching the news on TV (if that doesn't bother you), listening to music, or a soaking in a warm bathtub. Washing, brushing our teeth or having a hot drink – those things that we repeat day after day – lend a kind of comfort that will help our minds prepare for sleep.

Before finally settling down we should make sure we are going to be comfortable. If the nights are cool, a pair of flannel pajamas or nightgown will help keep us warm. An extra blanket with a little bit of weight to it can provide a cozy, safe feeling. And many a person has been kept awake by cold feet – a simple problem that a warm pair of socks could easily have cured.

If, in spite of all this care we've given ourselves, we still can't sleep after an hour or so of trying – or, if we've slept and woken in the middle of the night and can't get back to sleep – then it's time to get up for a while and do something. This is a far better option than tossing and turning.

Getting up and doing some small quiet jobs or reading – anything that does not require a lot of physical effort – makes the time we spend awake serve a useful purpose and helps us get our minds off our roaming thoughts. If we feel the need to express ourselves or sort out our thinking, writing in a journal would be extremely helpful. After an hour or so we will feel more relaxed and perhaps ready to settle down for sleep.

But remember: even if we don't actually sleep, conscious resting with our eyes closed can do a lot of good too. And, who knows? We may actually end up sleeping more than we think.

Combating Loneliness

The deepest need of man is the need to overcome his separateness,
to leave the prison of his aloneness.
– Erich Fromm, *The Art of Loving*

It feels good to be alone once in a while. Most of us enjoy the peace of solitude, reading a good book or listening to music. We often choose to be alone in order to have a holiday from busy activity and surroundings.

But there *is* an aloneness we all feel at times, an aloneness that is not so pleasant – that is not brought on by choice. This is the feeling of loneliness or isolation.

Many of us live on our own. If this is the case, home can be a lonely place, especially if we spend a lot of time there. For those who live alone, a dog or cat can provide good companionship. Pets are faithful and loving – they can help fill the empty rooms with their warm presence. The therapeutic value of pets is well recognized.

A lonely household could also benefit from having a radio or tape playing some of the time. There's no shortage of talk shows to keep us company and the selection of music available to us is endless.

Loneliness is a feeling of isolation, of not belonging, of always being out of touch. We do not have to be alone to be lonely. We can be lonely in a room full of people if we feel we don't fit in. We can feel lonely because we consider ourselves different from others. Even with many friends, it's possible to be lonely, simply because we don't feel very close to them.

Having a mood disorder increases our sense of loneliness, especially when we feel we have to keep it hidden. We tend to feel isolated in our differentness. We sense a lack of understanding, even in the family members and friends who love us.

Although we can never completely escape feelings of isolation, we can make the pain of our loneliness more bearable by taking time to relate to others. Through sharing freely our thoughts and feelings, whether they be happy or painful, we can break down the barriers between ourselves and others. Developing close friendships in which we're willing to make a commitment can help us deal with our isolation. Honest and sincere communication is the key. We must also remember that a good friendship is a two-way street. We should be willing to give as well as take. Relationships like these are precious – something we should strive to develop.

There are many places where we can find such friends. If we have an interest in hobbies or sports there are clubs and classes galore for us to join. Here we would meet others with interests similar to ours. Belonging to a church can open many opportunities to join in a variety of church-related groups and their activities.

Loneliness will always be with us to some degree, no matter how close we are to other people. We cannot change this fact. But we mustn't let loneliness become a tomb – encasing us. As we learn to reach out, even through such a simple act as waving to a neighbor, we will learn to minimize our isolation.

6

SUPPORTIVE RELATIONSHIPS

Supportive Relationships

No man is an island, entire of itself,
every man is a piece of the continent, a part of the main...
– John Donne, *Devotions upon Emergent Occasions*, 1624

Every one of us, whether we are healthy or whether we have an illness, needs to have a network of supportive relationships to help and encourage us with our day-to-day life. These relationships can range from spouse to friend, from medical professional to employer. Support can be found in churches and in self-help groups, in clubs and in schools.

It is wise to develop a wide range of these relationships. We need to have support in place in all areas of our life, not just for times when we need help, but also for when times are good. Becoming active in the community will help us meet people who could become important to us as friend or guide.

A supportive relationship provides us with someone we can call when we have a problem or when we need to talk to someone. We all need a shoulder to cry on now and then. There will be other times when we might reverse roles and offer a sympathetic ear to our friend.

Supportive friends can help us in practical ways now and again: supplying our emergency needs when we're sick, watering our plants when we're on holidays, comforting us when we need comforting.

People are social creatures and it is the nature of the society we live in that all its members depend on each other for the help they need to live and succeed. It would indeed be difficult to be completely autonomous. To thrive we must reach out to one another and benefit from what each of us has to offer.

Most friends welcome the opportunity to be of help once in a while. But we must be careful not to lean too heavily on them or take them for granted. Supportive relationships are valuable ones and we must always be grateful for them.

Care From the Heart –
A Special Kind of Support

"And how's my friend today?" Dr. McDougall's friendly voice asked as he came walking beside me down the hallway. He always brought a little brightness into the depressing surroundings of this psychiatric hospital ward.

Dr. McDougall usually made an effort to give a special hello. He was ready to talk to me if I felt able and needed to express myself. He encouraged me and showed he cared.

In later years, after I had left the hospital and Dr. McDougall had entered private practice, I continued to see him in his office.

He seemed almost as much a friend as a doctor. When I became sick while pregnant and had to go to hospital, I asked him if he would come to see me every day while I was there – probably a bit of an unreasonable request, I can see now. But he did come – every day!

Each lunch hour he took time to rush in, check with the nursing station and then with me. And, if he saw me drinking coffee, he'd scold me and tell me how bad it was for me. If I happened to look depressed, he expressed sincere concern. I don't know how anyone could have given better care, especially the way he did – straight from the heart.

Dr. McDougall moved away 20 years ago. But I've never totally said goodbye. When he told me he was leaving, he asked me to send him a card at Christmas. And I've been doing that every Christmas since, cards as well as letters. I like to write and tell him how things are – like an annual report – especially when good things happen to me. He usually returns the greeting and sometimes even a letter. It's good to know that Dr. McDougall is still there rooting for me.

Sometimes I wonder just how much influence this big-hearted doctor has had on my life. Somehow I feel that it may be far greater than I will ever know.

Family

The common hopes and interests and sorrows –
these create and sanctify the home.
– Sir John Lubbock

Our most important support usually comes from our family, the people who are closest to us. A spouse or other family member knows us better than anyone else. Those who live with us are often the first to detect symptoms when they arise and can help us to recognize them. Family members who have taken the effort to learn about our illness are in an especially good position to understand us and help.

The basic challenge of everyday living with a mood disorder makes support from family very important. It's good to have a loved one nearby to talk to when the need arises. We need their encouragement when things seem hopeless.

Having someone to help with the cooking and dishes is invaluable when we're down. In a beautiful way, the energy of our helper can rub off on us, helping us feel stronger for a while. Doing things is easier when it's not all up to us. Physical help is as important as emotional help.

Supporting a family member who has a mood disorder is not an easy thing, however. As the ones receiving the support, we should not take their help for granted. We should appreciate the hardships and sacrifices our illness often causes our family. When we have people who love us and who are willing to help watch out for us and care for us when we're not well, we are indeed very fortunate.

My Husband and Friend

I was a patient at Riverview Hospital two times: first, for a four-month period and then, a few months later, for a six-month stay.

It was during the in-between period that I met Wes. We gradually became friends, spending much time together.

When I was re-admitted to hospital a few months later he continued seeing me. Eventually, when I was allowed weekends at home, he spent most of this time with me: taking me to movies, the occasional party, and on numerous drives out of town. Sunday nights he returned me to the hospital. After a hug and a kiss, we knocked hard on the heavy locked door until someone let me back onto the ward.

Now I wasn't a pretty sight in those days – not somebody you'd be proud to show off to your friends. I was in a daze most of the time, partly due to the medications and partly because of the depression. I had become overweight (probably because mealtimes had become the highlight of these days that were filled with such boredom). My mouth hung open much of the time. But Wes never showed any shame of me. He never stopped believing in me. He never stopped being my friend. I was, and am to this day, a very fortunate person to have him by my side.

After three years of dating, we married. Wes didn't even have to ask me. Somehow we knew we were destined to spend our lives together.

Over the 27 years we've been married we've both had to learn how to get along with each other. Coping with my mood swings has not been easy for Wes. When I'm depressed he has difficulty too, often becoming somewhat depressed himself.

When I see that happen I try to boost his spirits. In the process I often boost my own a bit. At times living together becomes similar to playing on a seesaw in a children's playground. When I see that I'm pulling him down I struggle to come up. This is followed by his coming up and my dropping down again. And so it goes. By trying to help each other we both survive.

There have been occasional times of psychosis and paranoia when I haven't trusted people close to me. I even suspected Wes of plotting against me. Often I became overly anxious or simply irrational. But he has remained steadily by my side all these years.

Wes has learned to see the early symptoms of my illness when they arise and he warns me by gently pointing them out. I have gradually learned to respect his understanding of my illness and to listen to his warnings (most of the time anyway). Together, we try to get me back on track.

With a Little Help

Over recent years my husband has come to my aid when I'm so depressed that I have trouble doing even the most basic household jobs, such as shopping for groceries or cooking meals. These jobs may not seem like they would take much effort, but when I'm in the midst of depression they can seem insurmountable. One of the worst things about this is the feeling of guilt that comes with this seeming laziness.

Wes has learned to willingly join me in my tasks at times like this – I don't even need to ask. This help does a great deal for me. In an almost magical way I seem to absorb his energy so that the work becomes easier. As we shop and cook together there is a friendly interaction between us that is truly healing.

Receiving help like this also shows me that he understands what I'm going through. To be understood in this way is such a relief!

Friendship

What is the secret of making friends? There is no secret.
Friends, like all good things in this life, can be had by anyone
who wants them. There is only one simple rule to follow;
it is this: To have a friend, be one yourself.
– Author Unknown

Studies have shown that the social relationships we have in all the facets of our life – in our marriage, work, friendships, church, and clubs – are important for sustaining health. In these relationships we find friends to confide in, people we can trust. Talking over our troubles and sharing our joy with someone helps us to survive.

Friendship is the one special kind of support we should all seek. The most valuable of these relationships are those that have some depth to them. We need friends who know us well enough to be willing to spend time with us, to listen when we need to talk, and for whom we'll do the same.

Most of us cannot handle a lot of really close relationships like these. They require much time and intense sharing of emotions. Often a best friend is a husband or a wife.

Every friendship we have has its own unique qualities. One friend may make a better companion in certain situations than another person. We may have friends who can fill many different needs: for example, we may share a hobby with one, discuss child-raising problems with another, or discuss personal feelings with a third.

It's wise not to spend too much time alone. Whenever possible, talk with someone each day, even if it's only on the phone. A friendly voice and smile will go far toward helping us remember the bright side of life at times when we're threatened by depression. And when we're high, friends will help us keep things in perspective.

Spiritual Support

Our Father makes of us one family
One Infinite Great Love doth claim us all –
All one in him!
– John Oxenham, *We Are All Kin*

Anyone will tell you that a strong tree needs to have a healthy root system to survive – to grow. The root supports of some trees are as widespread underground as the branches are above. They need to be continually nourished with food and water.

Storms may come and these trees won't be uprooted. Drought may come, but the roots reach deep to the water stored below. The tree may experience difficulties, but it will not die.

That's the way it is with our spiritual lives and the spiritual roots of the families we come from. These firm roots helped our forebears have the strength they needed, under great adversity, to explore and settle in a wild land. In those early days, their spiritual faith helped them cope with the challenging problems life presented to them. At that time, the place of worship was the center of the community.

It's unfortunate but true that in this modern world spirituality has disappeared from the lives of many. Over the years many roots have been severed. Most don't know or realize the generous support a community church, synagogue, or temple can offer us as we try to cope with the problems life presents to us.

Friends with whom we hold a common belief could be the most valuable ones we'll have. They can help us solve our problems from a common perspective.

Self-help Groups

I get by with a little help from my friends.
– John Lennon and Paul McCartney

As awareness about mental illness grows, self-help groups are becoming more and more common, both to serve those who have an illness and for members of their family. These groups are now active in increasingly more towns and cities throughout Canada and the U.S.

Self-help groups should not, and usually don't, involve professionals. They are organized and run solely by individuals who have mood disorders. Meetings are held on a regular basis: usually once a week or once a month.

Self-help groups for people with mood disorders offer a safe place to talk about our struggles with others whose experiences are similar and who are able to understand us. Here we can share freely without fear of stigma. In the process, we learn to be more comfortable while talking to others about our illness. Talking with others who have problems not unlike ours takes away some of the feelings of isolation that are so often a part of our lives. It is freeing to be able to speak to those who understand, relieving some of the burden we have when we're forced to keep a secret. We come to realize that there are many others in the world, suffering as we are. We're not alone.

At group meetings we have an opportunity to compare notes on the latest medications. We can express frustrations we may feel about our treatment. It is a place to exchange information. Here we find people who will encourage and support us. When we're having trouble identifying our problems, the group can help us identify them and help work out a solution.

Self-help groups offer the opportunity to make friends and socialize with people we have something in common with. Some groups become like families, which is especially valuable if emotional support at home is lacking. They're places where we can count on being accepted and treated with respect. Meeting as equals with others who share problems similar to our own does much to raise our self-esteem.

The Telephone

I want to apologize for plaguing you with so many telephone calls
last November and December. When the "enthusiasm" is coming on me
it is accompanied by a feverish reaching to my friends.
After it's over I wince and wither.
– Robert Lowell, in a letter to T. S. Eliot, March 1964

One of the lesser-known symptoms of mood disorders is excessive use of the telephone. This would be good to remember when we find ourselves making call after call to one friend and the next.

When we're high we're excited about all the thoughts that come to us: the things we've read, the thoughts we've had. They're just too precious to keep to ourselves. We want to reach out to our friends immediately. Sometimes this means that we're phoning as early as 6:00 in the morning and sometimes as late as 1:00 at night. Our judgment is very poor.

Some of us withdraw when we're depressed, but some individuals (like me) want to be in touch with our friends during these times as well. We need to be assured of their love. But we tend to cling too much.

If we could put ourselves in our friends' shoes (actually a very difficult thing to do at times like this) we would see that many find these constant phone calls too much. Although they love us, most are busy and can't afford to spend a lot of time on the phone, especially when we call several times a day. This is true for even the dearest of friends.

Why not try to keep a little journal in which to make entries of things we would like to tell each of our friends? We could then refer to it when we talk to them in person or when we make an occasional phone call.

If we have a spiritual faith that's strong, prayer could also be very helpful when we need to talk.

Journaling

When you have shut your doors and darkened your room,
remember never to say that you are alone; for God is within,
and your genius is within,
and what need have they of light to see what you are doing?
– Epictetus (c.50–120)

There *will* be times when friends are out of reach. Late at night, when we can't sleep, is often the time we're most anxious and when we most have the need to talk.

A journal could be a very good friend at a time like this. "Talking" daily (or whenever we feel we'd like to) to a journal helps us sort things out.

It's been said that thoughts kept in our head tend not to reach conclusions – they just go round and round, not stopping, seldom settling on anything. When we write down our concerns, it's more likely that we'll be able to deal satisfactorily with them. Just setting them down on paper helps – we no longer need to keep our minds busy with them.

We can use our journal in a wide variety of ways. We can "talk" to it every night – reviewing how the day went, expressing what bothered or pleased us, making resolutions for the future, writing poems, writing prayers, copying down quotes that impress us, copying the words to a song that we find meaningful, sketching, saving clippings from magazines and newspapers.

There's no end to what kind of journal we can keep. It can be our personal and unique expression of what we are all about.

A journal provides a way to look back to check on our past mood swings. It's possible to track the ups and downs, something which could aid in making decisions for future treatment.

Reading over past entries can be very revealing. We might be amazed at the feelings we had two or three months ago. Reading about them will help us remember and learn from them.

7

A SPIRITUAL SOURCE OF STRENGTH

Spirituality

...our spiritual life is the life of the Spirit of God within us...
Although it is very hard to control our moods,
we can gradually overcome them by a well-disciplined spiritual life...
if we spend some time reading the Gospels, praying the Psalms,
and thanking God for a new day,
our moods may lose their power over us.
– Henri J. M. Nouwen

Like a mother hen sitting on her brood of eggs, not moving except to turn them once in a while, we often brood; we become almost inactive. Our brain tosses around thoughts: worry thoughts, wondering thoughts, good thoughts, bad thoughts. Yet we protect this inner busyness from the world – not communicating, not joining with the bustle of everyday living. Our breathing slows down. The real world becomes more and more distant.

Although we don't really feel depressed at first, withdrawal such as this could signal the beginning of a depressed period. We should try not to allow this mood to escalate and take hold.

This is where those who have a faith have an advantage over those who don't. Those who believe in God can, in cases like this, try to replace this inward talk that is addressed to no one but themselves with talk that is addressed to God. Instead of allowing their thoughts to go around in circles and pull them deeper and deeper within, they can, through prayer, talk to God. In "talking" their wishes, fears, and problems out in this way, these thoughts are released into God's care. The brooding no longer paralyzes us.

If we held such a belief, we could, in a mood of impending darkness like this, turn to our ability to pray and to accept friends' prayers. We no longer need to hang on to problems and fears all by ourselves. The weight on us is lifted. Gradually we recapture an active, positive feeling. It becomes easier to laugh. We want to be with our friends again.

The beauty of the out-of-doors regains its clarity. The plastic sheath that seemed to cover the world has lifted and the colors of the grass and trees are an emerald green once more.

Faith

...but those who hope in the Lord
will renew their strength.
They will soar on wings like eagles;
they will run and not grow weary,
they will walk and not be faint.
– Isaiah 40:31

Remember when we were children, playing in the playground, hanging on as tightly as possible from the highest rung of the monkey bars? We were afraid of falling. Our hands gripped the metal bar firmly; we felt panicky. Our dad stood below, encouraging us to let go, reassuring us that he would catch us.

Many of us would cling to our fear, not trusting our father. The rest of us would be relieved and would be able to let go of the bar, allowing ourselves to drop into his strong waiting arms. To have faith (or to let go of anxiety) should be so easy and yet, because of our lack of trust, it is often so incredibly hard.

Faith is a remarkable thing; it can be a medicine for the spirit. Whether we have faith in a person, thing, truth, or God, trusting something or somebody outside of ourselves can create a sense of confidence and peace within us. Distrust, on the other hand, brings with it feelings of anxiety. To have faith we need to loosen our tight grip on this anxiety and let go. This "letting go" will help us to counteract stress in our day-to-day life and also at times of crisis.

Having faith in someone who cares for us is to believe that this person is trustworthy, understands us, and has our interest at heart. To have faith is to give up the idea that we have to do everything on our own and to accept another's help. Having faith is to stop our anxious struggling and to rest in the assurance that things will work out. This is how many of us have found spiritual belief to be a great source of comfort and strength. Faith in God provides a quiet optimism which brings peace of mind.

It follows that faith in our doctors and the medications they give us is vital if they are to help us effectively. It is important to find a doctor we feel comfortable with, someone who cares for us and accepts us, someone we can trust. Though this sense of trust will probably take some time to build, it should be our aim.

It's also important to learn about the medications that are available. When we have learned what medications can or cannot do for us, it becomes easier to believe in their usefulness and to take them regularly.

Studies have shown that patients who have a spiritual faith and, in turn, a high level of trust in their doctor and treatment have a greater chance at becoming well.

The strange thing is that, by resting in our faith, by letting go of our anxiety, we build confidence and strength. By learning to let go of sole reliance on ourselves, we actually gain the courage to do more.

Overload

My problems are usually greatest when several stressful events come together at one time. I become overloaded.

On one occasion like this several years ago, at a time before I was taking a mood stabilizer, I had become quite manic. Strong emotion went into everything I did and I got myself involved in more projects than I could manage.

I was doing freelance photography for the local newspaper, for the school board, and the health department. Many of the projects were self-assigned. They were the products of ideas that arose one after another because of my manic state.

One project was to candidly photograph the backstage activities at a dance festival. A second one that I dreamed up was to photograph, candidly, the interaction between able-bodied children with disabled children. I wanted to illustrate the caring spirit many young children have – more than many give them credit for. Then there was the photo essay I did featuring my elderly father-in-law while he was in an extended care hospital.

I worked very hard on all these projects and was happy (in fact, ecstatic) about how the photos turned out. It was an odd feeling when, only two weeks after the photo session with him, my father-in-law died. I'd used, without realizing it at the time, my last opportunity to photograph him.

The photos I took at the dance festival also turned out well and resulted in a full-page photo essay in the newspaper and an invitation from the provincial arts festival to be their official photographer the following year.

The photos I shot of able-bodied children with disabled children at an elementary school were very emotional for me. I was pleased when both the school board publication and the paper prepared stories to accompany the pictures.

With all these successful and emotional events coming so closely together, I became very stressed. Gradually I became psychotic. It became difficult to function.

The case of my father-in-law's death coming so shortly after my intensive photo session seemed too much a coincidence. (This was only one of several amazing coincidences that I've had over the years.) Somehow, especially at that point of my life, I had to admit that God must have had a hand in it, though I had long ago rejected Christianity as a teenager.

But now I felt God's strong presence and wanted to accept Jesus as part of my life. I decided to give up trying to battle the ups and downs entirely on my own and began to lean on my newfound faith. Although my conversion to Christianity did not happen all at once, a sense of peace gradually replaced the anxiety that I had suffered as part of my illness.

Soon after this critical period, my doctor prescribed the mood stabilizer, lithium, for me. This helped me keep a better balance. The better medication, together with my newly found faith, made my life easier to cope with. In the past I had often lost my temper with my husband and son, with nasty yelling and screaming. Now, although there are as many crises in my life as there used to be, I'm handling them better.

Becoming a Christian has done wonders for how I approach life. My creative work has taken on new meaning. I've found a useful purpose for it. I now want to use my talents to serve my community in a more meaningful way.

Faith at Times of Depression

Although my faith is normally strong, it seems as if, when I most need it, I can't rely on it. I usually believe in my abilities, in a positive future, in God. However, these beliefs often disappear during deep depression. Dark doubts turn into a black feeling of hopelessness.

If only I could hang on to my faith better at times like these! It's when I manage to keep the ability to pray that I find the comfort I need so much. But it's the nature of depression to rob us of the ability to see the positive – to keep us from being hopeful.

I hang on as well as I can and, as I begin to pick up again, my faith gradually returns – and with it, the desire to carry on.

To Be a Butterfly

God give me courage to trust
I can break my chrysalis too!
– Alice Freeman Palmer, *The Butterfly*

There is much we can learn from nature about coping with life. We can look at the ebb and flow of the tides and see how that phenomenon is reflected in our lives. The sharp contrasts that are part of our lives echo those seen in nature. The darkness of night is always followed by the light of day; and after the storm, the sun comes out. In a beautiful way the workings of nature seem to parallel what happens in our lives.

There is one symbol I've adopted from nature that I've found immensely helpful when I'm into my "down" times. I read once how the life cycle of a butterfly resembles mood swings. The emergence of a butterfly from its cocoon stage, the chrysalis, is similar to our recovery from depression.

The chrysalis hangs lifelessly, wrapped in a casing that makes movement difficult. But the creature inside the chrysalis is patient, waiting for the transformation that will occur – knowing that its shell will soon break open to reveal a colorful, carefree butterfly.

When I keep this butterfly image firmly fixed in my mind, coping with depression becomes less difficult. I still feel low on energy and enthusiasm, but now I have faith that my brighter self will appear again. This tends to give me a sense of peace. Patiently I try to bide my time, doing whatever I can manage to do. The healing comes a little easier.

Patience

Patience is not passive: on the contrary it is active;
it is concentrated strength.
– Author Unknown

We often hear the word "patience" used in connection with doing a craft, or learning to play an instrument, or any activity that takes a large amount of concentrated effort in order to accomplish only a small amount. We talk about having patience as if it were a God-given ability – something not everyone is endowed with.

But much patience can be learned: learned by trusting our own ability to make our effort pay off (all in good time), by trusting that the seemingly impossible *is* possible. We learn to believe that what we're trying to accomplish *can* and *will* be accomplished by quietly pursuing our goals with determination.

Patience will allow us to plant our seeds and, with confidence, give them time to sprout and grow.

So it is with the patience we need to recover from a bout of depression. We learn to maintain an attitude of quiet waiting – a belief that "this too will pass." This requires us to "go with it" – to not fight it too hard, but to accept that we're ill and that, with the medications our doctor has prescribed, our illness *will* pass.

If we're taking a new medication we need to have patience to allow it to kick in. Sometimes medication takes effect immediately – sometimes it takes six or more weeks. Best to trust your doctor when needing further advice.

Hope

Hope ever urges us on, and tells us tomorrow will be better.
– Albius Tibullus (c.54–19 BC)

To have hope is to have a healthy, positive belief in ourselves and in our future. Hope instills in us an energy to work toward something better.

If we are to maintain this optimistic attitude, it is important to keep ourselves active. It is only through actively moving ahead with purpose that we can keep our hope flourishing. To spend hours in unproductive idleness, on the other hand, tends to lead to a feeling of futility and despair.

When we are depressed or when we experience a severe illness, our inactivity causes our belief in the future to become dim. Our ability to function and to move forward is disrupted and it becomes difficult to believe in a better tomorrow. In our overall life, a good positive attitude is invaluable. We need to believe optimistically in future possibilities for ourselves.

We should, as often as possible, spend part of our days doing activities we truly enjoy. Even if we don't like the job we have, most of us *do* have spare time that we can use for hobbies or other activities. We all need to do things we really love doing or things we truly believe in. If we know that, at the end of the day or the week, we have something fun or something meaningful waiting for us to do, we'll have hope in our lives.

While we are well, we are more capable of the hopeful thinking we need to build our skills and plant the seeds of opportunity. If we can combine positive thinking with positive action, we'll have a life filled with hope, a life filled with promise. Then, when depression strikes, it may not bend us as low as it otherwise would.

When depression *does* come and we lose confidence, remember that the negative feeling is due to our illness and is only temporary. Faithful acceptance will help us to patiently allow it to run its course. We can pick things up again where we left off when we're better. It may sometimes be hard to believe, but a new day always dawns.

Hope for Our Children

Not so long ago, when I was a young child in the 1950s, medications for psychiatric illnesses were only beginning to be developed. Thus, when I was first sick in my late teens in the 1960s there were few drugs for the doctors to choose from to treat me and my fellow patients. Research had been done, but not nearly as much as today.

And now, here I am in the late 1990s, and great strides have been made in the understanding of my illness and the medications to treat it. I find this truly amazing – and am sincerely grateful to all who've brought psychiatry this far.

Dozens of organizations have sprung up to meet the needs of people with illnesses such as mine. There are self-help groups, drop-in centers, job-training programs, and a collection of other services which have our interests at heart.

Of course, much still has to be muddled through. Our society still has the burden of finding sufficient support for the many ill people who live on the streets, those who themselves don't understand they're sick and in desperate need of medical care. Much needs to be done to cure those shortcomings of our medical care system. We who know and understand the nature of illnesses such as manic depression and schizophrenia must help in that battle. Those of us who understand and feel compassion must cry out for better treatment of those that seem to be forgotten by family and friends.

Mental illness is not a popular sickness. Governments spend less money on research and care for this than for almost any other illness. In 1992, in one piece of literature, the Canadian Mental Health Association (B.C. Division) stated that, "...for every person with cancer, $400 is spent on research whereas only $11 is spent on research for each person living with schizophrenia."

Nevertheless, there are indications that the stigma associated with mental illness for centuries is gradually being stripped away and, with it, the blind eye that society has for so long had for our problems. Many individuals, with the depressive disorders in particular, are openly telling their stories, no longer ashamed to reveal what they used to keep secret.

Hope is evident in the field of psychiatry. Medical staff, researchers, patients and their families – all who care – must now work to keep the ball of positive action rolling. I can truly see a better day for our children and grandchildren.

Forgiving Others and Ourselves

Bear with each other and forgive whatever grievances you may have against one another. Forgive as the Lord forgave you.
– Colossians 3:13

We all store up so many unresolved problems: conflicts between ourselves and others that make us angry, or mistakes we ourselves have made that we're sorry about but still keep kicking ourselves for. Whenever we think of these old angers, they cause us stress and we feel miserable. They feed the negative thinking that is part of depression.

To relieve these bad feelings we need to resolve the problem by trying to put ourselves in the place of the person who has hurt or wronged us. We need to recognize that he or she is human too and can make mistakes as we ourselves make mistakes. To be happy and healthy we must adopt a forgiving spirit. If we could learn to understand others and forgive them, it would become possible to let go of the past and to be free to feel love toward our adversary again. The weight of bitterness would be lifted from our minds.

One of the worst feelings that haunts us is the needless anger we direct at ourselves for the mistakes we're sorry for – for those "stupid" things we wished we'd never done or said. For those with mood disorders, this presents a worse difficulty than it does for others because of our frequent problems with poor judgment. Our mood swings often cause us to do things we normally wouldn't do – things we're later ashamed of.

We must, however, learn to forgive ourselves – as the Bible says God forgives – and accept that we are human and have problems. If we can accept this forgiveness, we can be free to live with self-assurance. We will have to maintain *some* reservation to guard us from repeating our mistakes too often. But by accepting ourselves and liking ourselves, in spite of it all, we can stop harboring persistent blame and anger.

When our thoughts constantly turn back to angry, hateful, or regretful memories, we waste a lot of energy on negative feelings. By learning to forgive ourselves and others we make it possible to love more freely and sincerely. And love brings happiness and healing.

Love

> *Love is patient, love is kind... It always protects,*
> *always trusts, always hopes, always perseveres.*
> – 1 Corinthians 13:4, 7

We all depend on relationships for our happiness and growth. We need to love and be loved. Love for others warms and brightens our hearts and melts away feelings of hardness and bitterness. When we are able to love fully, our attitudes toward those around us are softened – we do not blame but only look at the good in others.

If we can forgive others their faults and love unconditionally by giving and accepting freely, our lives become truly precious. When we learn to love like this we tend to forget about our own desires and needs while we reach outside ourselves and focus on others. When we're interested in others, we think less about our own illness. This kind of love is very healing.

A love like this will inspire us to do things for others, to help those who are less fortunate. When we learn to love freely we'll find the ability within us to be compassionate and helpful when someone is suffering. We'll discover that we have much more to give than we had imagined.

Probably the most important ingredient of a loving relationship is good communication. To become truly close to another person we need to be sincere and honest with them. It's important to express our feelings and to be interested in our friend's feelings. This breaks down the walls between individuals and builds trust, security, and satisfaction for both parties.

Love is not something to be quietly hidden in our hearts. It will not grow there but will eventually die. Love needs to be brought into the light of our day-to-day lives and exercised. We can express our love by smiling at the people we meet, showing an interest in others, searching out friends for a visit.

We need to tell others how we feel about them – a difficult thing to do when we're not accustomed to expressing our feelings, but something we *can* get used to doing. (Try it with a greeting card to begin with. Saying "I love you" is easier to do in writing.)

Giving love means that we'll also reap the rewards of receiving love. There is great joy in both the giving *and* receiving. Sharing our love with others helps to reduce not only others' loneliness, but our own as well. It will help us feel whole, peaceful, happy.

Being Grateful

Gratitude is heaven itself.
– William Blake

Remember the old song about falling asleep "counting your blessings"? Counting our blessings or, for many people, thanking God through prayer, has long been recognized as a very healing exercise.

Being grateful helps us focus on the positive elements of our life and minimize the negative. No matter how dim our lot may be at times, there are always things to be thankful for. When we take time to think about our good fortunes, one at a time, the resulting mood change can be significant.

For example, we could think of our bodies and each part that works, and count them a blessing, a blessing which makes us very fortunate. We may not be feeling very happy, but our eyes can see and our legs can walk – abilities not everyone has and ones we shouldn't take for granted. It's healthy now and then to spend some time savoring all we're grateful for – even going so far as making a list.

Taking time to consider our good fortunes can elevate our mood level to "heaven itself," as William Blake put it. It's truly amazing how much joy the simple exercise of reviewing our blessings can bring.

Counting My Blessings, A sample list

- I have my sight.
- I have my hearing.
- I have so much music I can listen to – music I love – whenever I want.
- I'm free to walk – in the parks in my neighborhood and elsewhere.
- There are many fun and beautiful things to see that I can be grateful for: the squirrels, bounding across the road, gathering food; the crows, with their wise (yes, wise) antics; the trees, the grasses, and the shrubbery, each a different hue of green.
- I have friends and family members who love me and care for me.
- We live in a country in which we're free to worship in any way we wish.
- I have food to eat.

- I have a comfortable bed on which to sleep and dream.
- I have the preciousness of life, a life that begins anew with every morning.

Joy In the Midst of Agony

Several years ago, under the supervision of my doctor, I tried to come off the anti-psychotic drug I'd been taking for many years. It was beginning to cause dangerous side effects and we thought it important to change medications.

But this was not an easy thing to do. I became sick and was psychotic for several weeks. Against my doctor's wishes I denied myself the fully prescribed dose of the drug.

I became housebound, not well enough to venture out. My functioning was heavily impaired – I could do very little. I became paranoid, mistrusting one or two of the people closest to me. The long days became like a nightmare; they were hard to bear.

But my friends rallied around me, my family lovingly showed they cared, and my faith in God remained steadfast. All th   helped sustain me.

I remember a particular occasion during this stormy period: One after-noon, while sitting on my bed, (my favorite place of seclusion), I decided I'd like to thank God for all God had given me. Because the long hours were filled with such misery, I felt a need to touch base with something positive. In spite of the suffering I was undergoing, I had clung to the belief that, beyond my illness, I had a life to be grateful for.

I bowed my head and, one at a time, brought to mind each friend who meant a lot to me. I slowly meditated on all the things I loved about them. I thought of times we had shared together. Then I thanked God for each in turn and asked God to bless them.

My mind went to beautiful places and things I had seen and appreciated. Pictures of them appeared in my memory one at a time, and I slowly allowed myself to roam around in them, enjoying each detail. For each image I gave thanks to God.

Gradually, after a long period of these prayers, I became filled with an intense joy. I had been consumed by agony; yet now I felt elation.

It hasn't always been so easy to be grateful when all seemed hopeless. I try, but have difficulty. Yet in some phases of illness, joy can still come from focusing on the positive.

And, during good times, I often feel my heart dance inside me when I thank God for all I've received. My entire being celebrates.

The Positive Side of Suffering

Character cannot be developed in ease and quiet.
Only through experience of trial and suffering can the soul be strengthened,
vision cleared, ambition inspired, and success achieved.
– Helen Keller, *Helen Keller's Journal*

Although we don't wish ourselves or anyone else to undergo physical, emotional or mental suffering, the experience is not altogether bad for us. Suffering enriches our character. We learn to understand others who suffer; we learn to have compassion.

Carl Jung spoke of the "wounded healer." The person who has courageously survived their own ordeal with a disease can return, empowered to help others in their healing process. There's no one as well equipped to help someone in distress as the person who has been in a similar situation. The great effectiveness of the self-help groups that have become so popular bear witness to Jung's theory.

Those who have suffered greatly and then recover usually appreciate the value of their lives more than those who have not needed to struggle. They come to look on life as a rich gift, which should not be taken for granted. They're thankful for their wellness and try to use it wisely. It's no coincidence that many of history's greatest personalities have had a background filled with struggle.

After the Pain

I have been sick many times and have suffered greatly. But, although it was no fun, I can't say I regret having gone through these trials. Without them I wouldn't be as full a person as I am – and I probably wouldn't value my life as much as I do.

Each time I get sick and then recover, my recovery is like the dawning of a new day. Each time I go through the pain of psychosis, I come out of it having learned new lessons about life. I gradually "awaken" from each ill period bearing a new perspective, a fresh attitude, and a greater appreciation for what it means to be alive.

After years of ups and downs, I've learned thoroughly how it feels to be depressed, manic, and psychotic. It's easier for me to understand what others go through when they're down. It's easier to be sympathetic and to know what to do to help.

For example, I feel that I understand somewhat the difficulty elderly people living in institutions face – the loneliness they must feel. I care about them and, in small ways try to help by being part of a group of church members who visit shut-ins. Sometimes I publish little inspirational booklets and, through stories and poems, I try to help them with the feelings they must be experiencing. I probably wouldn't be doing things like that if I hadn't been ill and in hospitals myself.

Suffering will always be a part of my life, as it is part of everyone's life. It's not something I wish for. But when it comes, it's a consolation if I can remember that this pain provides just another building block in my life – something that will, in the end, help make a more complete person out of me. Suffering will take its toll, but when I recover, it's possible to rise and face the day with renewed vigor.

Moving Beyond Ourselves

We make a living by what we get,
but we make a life by what we give.
– Norman MacEwan

The most important form of therapy we can engage in is to reach beyond ourselves – beyond working solely for our own personal gain. Acting for the sake of someone we care about or for a cause that we believe in takes us out of the victim role – both in our own eyes and in the eyes of others. In doing so, we take the opportunity to do for others instead of sitting back and waiting for others to do for us. No longer do we feel like a powerless, defeated person. We begin to look on our life as a victory.

Albert Schweitzer spoke of a moral principle involving what he called "good fortune obligates." It was his belief that those of us who have more than others in health, talents, ability, or any other gifts, must share these with those who are less fortunate. This principle could apply to each one of us – because everyone has something unique that they could share with someone else. Everyone has something they can offer that could help another person.

All of us are surrounded by people and groups of people who have needs. In fact, there is no individual who is without a need. We all need people to talk to, to work and play with. We all need help at times. An older person might need a hand with shopping or with a trip to the doctor. A blind person may need someone to read for them or to write the occasional letter. Thousands of people in hospitals and institutions are lonely, hungering for some individual attention, for a real friend. Food banks need fund raisers, a nonprofit organization needs a secretary, an environmental association needs a photographer. Maybe we ourselves can recognize where help is needed – help which hasn't even been asked for. Maybe we ourselves can see a situation that could be improved. And maybe we are just the right person for that task.

The ways in which people can reach beyond themselves and help others are as numerous as the number of people who have gifts to share and the thousands of ideas these people might, together, come up with. The more we use our imagination to dream up ideas for sharing what we have, the richer our power to give will become.

A teenage boy, on an unexpected impulse, shovels his neighbor's driveway. Each year, a family invites two or three people who are alone to have Christmas dinner with them. A young man with only one leg and a prosthesis hobbles his way across Canada to raise awareness of the need for cancer research. Creative giving exhilarates and rewards the giver *and* the receiver.

It feels good to have something to give and to give it – generously, freely – without expecting anything more than satisfaction in return. When we start helping others by giving of ourselves, we will find that we'll like ourselves better. Our self-esteem will be healthier.

The Golden Rule: "Do unto others as you would have them do unto you" has been a tried and true way to mental health. We have all heard the stories of men and women who have turned their lives with disabilities into lives filled with generous and inspired contribution to their community. Often, those who have disability in one area so value the abilities they *do* have that they strive hard to do all they can to make those abilities count for something. These "disadvantaged" individuals have made some of the most meaningful and valuable contributions to society.

When we engage ourselves in helping others, our focus turns away from ourselves. Our own struggles do not seem nearly as big when we see them next to the struggles other people undergo.

Giving to others in our personal lives, or as a volunteer working for an organization, will pay large dividends by leaving us with a sense of accomplishment – a sense of having done something worthwhile. We should realize that anything we contribute – large or small; whether in the home, the workplace, or the community – will have some form of impact on other people's welfare. And, as our giving increases, our happiness is also bound to grow. There's no better way to attain mental well-being.

Christmas Day

It was Christmas Day but I had to stay behind at the hospital. Only a few patients were left on the ward, those who like me, were not well enough to go home to their families. In the hollow quiet of the empty room we each opened a little gift. I got a string of big old-fashioned beads. It was kind of disappointing. I was only 19 years old, yet the necklace looked like it should belong to a grandmother.

Outside the seagulls were squawking lustfully, trying to get at the garbage in the bags piled below. I stood at the window and watched them. They were so alive – so free. Their cries reminded me of the seashore.

A nurse spoke from behind me, saying, "Why don't you feed them a little?" She opened the narrow window behind the bars and handed me a few slices of bread. A breath of freshness hit my face and I gasped at the shock of it. But slowly I relaxed and took one or two more deep breaths of the wonderful cool air. Then I broke the bread and held the pieces out for the birds, one at a time. They swooped and shrilly laid claim to the morsels, taking them from my hand. The air stirred with wings and echoes of wild cries.

And so, reaching beyond the iron bars, I fed these free and crazy creatures – and they ate. I helped to fill their empty stomachs. And did that ever feel great!

Gershwin Reflections

The radio softly played Gershwin's Rhapsody in Blue as I lay in bed trying to settle down for sleep. The familiar music brought back feelings and memories of days in my teens when I used to listen to it on my bed, transported by the power of it. Because my record collection was small at that time I ended up playing this frequently.

In those days I closeted myself in my bedroom whenever I could – away from my family and the boarders who shared our home – alone in my precious, private world. I used to read and think and daydream quite a bit, but did very little to make things happen. I watched the world outside from my silent vantage point, not entering into the vitality of it – remaining an outsider. The girl I was then was not a happy one.

Then I became sick and lost many months to psychosis as a patient in a mental hospital. I recovered well enough to be discharged, but it took a number of years to really rehabilitate. During those years I worked hard to become a fully functioning person again. As I struggled, it occurred to me that there must have been something wrong with the way I had been living. I gradually recognized that I needed to put something into the world instead of always taking from it. I realized that life is a precious gift, and that if I were grateful, I should use my skills and talents to give something back.

Today, as I lie here with the familiar music teasing the memories of that painful past, I ponder how different my life has become. My attitude is now the opposite of what it was in my youth. Today I actively work on meaningful projects. Reading and listening to music are still activities I enjoy, but what is most important to me is to make things of my own, to share what I think and feel with others, and to contribute to the community around me.

I have learned to be a doer instead of merely an observer. I have come out of my little room and become part of a bigger world. I am healthier: happy and fulfilled.

8

BUILDING CONFIDENCE

Building Confidence

The quality of life is determined by its activities.
– Aristotle (384–322 BC), *Nicomachean Ethics*

When we've suffered from a breakdown or recurring depression – when we're so often faced with feelings of inadequacy because our illness gets in the way of living a normal life – we tend to lose confidence in ourselves. It's not hard to become discouraged when life is difficult. The stigma attached to our illness pulls us down further, making us feel like an outcast.

As we will see in this section, there is much we can do to build a rewarding life for ourselves. We'll probably have to begin slowly, one step at a time. It may be difficult to begin to focus, but it *is* possible. One of the most inspiring people in history, the great composer Ludwig von Beethoven, teaches us a great lesson in what can be done in spite of severe disability. While completely deaf he created one of his best compositions, his *Ninth Symphony*. If *he* was able to accomplish what he did, what might be possible for *us*?

Each of us has a unique way of experiencing our illness. As our life progresses, we become familiar with how it manifests itself from day-to-day. We begin to recognize the symptoms and learn to manage them and get them under control. In the process we learn what we are able to do and not able to do – we learn what our limitations are.

Within the life we lead, however rocky, there is room for courageous building, with work and activities that will make us feel happy. How much we achieve is not the important thing. (The greatest achievers in the world are not necessarily the happiest people.) Simply doing the best we can with what we have will bring satisfaction and contentment. The important thing is to always keep moving forward and to use our time well to create a happy life.

We will gain self-confidence when we pursue activities with such vigor that we become good at what we do.

It doesn't matter *what* we do – as long as we do our best and do it with love. (Of course, it's pretty difficult to do our best at something we don't really love.)

Whether we learn to play the violin or become a painter, whether we learn computer magic or devote ourselves to teaching children, if we do our best at something our self-confidence will thrive.

Each morning presents new opportunities and challenging activities to explore and make the most of. This morning might be the time to begin an activity we'd only dreamed about.

All the mistakes and tough times of yesterday lie behind us and we can begin afresh to carve out a life for ourselves. Yes, we *will* have to make some allowances for our health; we need to keep ourselves in balance and we will have to take care of ourselves when we recognize the onset of symptoms. But those rules are true for almost any individual. Few people live without some kind of illness or disability.

The Importance of Being Active

> *Action may not always bring happiness:*
> *but there is no happiness without action.*
> – Benjamin Disraeli

One of the reasons for the awful way we feel when we're depressed is the lethargy which is such a big part of it. It's hard to be happy when we're feeling lazy. When I have a cold I feel so bad that I slow down to a crawl. I lie around, not feeling up to doing very much at all. At times like this I get depressed. It's the inactivity that brings it on.

Physical activity brings with it a sense of life and exhilaration. To stop planning and to actually start pursuing a goal is exciting; it makes us feel vibrant. Even the simple acts of carrying out our daily jobs and chores can bring with them a sense of satisfaction and contentment. It's vital always to try to maintain enough of this activity to keep us buoyed up.

Activity gives us a sense of control, resulting in happiness; inactivity brings a sense of helplessness and results in boredom and misery.

While we are well, keeping busy on a day-to-day basis will provide us with the balance we need to help keep depression at bay. We could alternate our more passive activities, such as reading and watching TV, with activities of a more physical nature: cooking, playing sports, or working on a job or hobby.

And when depression *does* become a threat, when the old familiar feelings of lethargy begin again, it's beneficial to try to increase our work and play, concentrating especially on what we really enjoy. If the depression hasn't taken hold yet, it may be a good time to work on the new project you've been eager to begin. The enthusiasm you have for the work you do might minimize or even prevent the depression from taking over.

When we become truly depressed, however, it's truly hard to be active. Pursuing ambitious goals is out of the question at times like this. But we can feel better by doing even small jobs; they can alleviate the depression. We must keep trying – to make our bodies move, even when our spirits don't want to. During times like this, it helps to keep our goals for the day simpler than normal, bearing in mind that we have low energy and need time to recharge. As long as we do whatever we can, we deserve to feel proud of ourselves.

Rise, Check Your Diary, and Shine!

You wake up in the morning, and lo!
your purse is magically filled with twenty-four hours of
the magic tissue of the universe of your life.
– Arnold Bennett

Whether we wake up looking forward to having a friend come for coffee or to going to a job, having a purpose for our day is important if we're going to wake up bright and happy. It's when we haven't anything to look forward to that even the most healthy and "normal" person ends up sleeping in and wasting the most precious minutes and hours of their day.

Unfortunately, many of us begin our days with a sense of aimlessness. We are in a bit of a fog as to how to use the time we have ahead of us. All too often we approach any goals we have half-heartedly. The good intentions we had the night before seem to be forgotten with the beginning of a new day. We pull the covers over our heads and try to hide from the sunshine streaming in the window. There seems to be nothing to get up for.

There *is* a way of creating better mornings for ourselves. Activity is one of the basic ingredients for happiness. Writing down the things we want to accomplish can provide an excellent way to spur ourselves to activity. If we keep a written list and refer to it often, we can effectively increase our motivation. Setting down goals on paper gives us a way to physically manifest things that have previously been only abstract thoughts floating around in our heads. By writing down what we intend to do, we can take the first step to the realization of our goals – and get a feeling of commitment.

Being a work-at-home person, I had to learn to be a self-starter – not always an easy thing to do. A few years ago, however, I began something that has greatly improved my own tendency to an aimless approach to the morning. I bought myself a planning diary and started writing down in detail each item I wanted to accomplish. This diary has made a dramatic difference to my life. Now, every evening before I go to bed, I list what I would like to do the next day: for example, ironing, grocery shopping, some specific work on my business, work on a hobby, a visit with a friend. I've learned to allow time for chores and also to make sure I always include some things I love to do. Wherever possible, I schedule activities that will lead me toward my more major goals. The ideal day I plan for myself should be an enticing one.

As I complete each item in my diary, I put a check beside it. Making those check marks gives me a feeling of satisfaction, a sense of achievement. If I don't get some things done, that's usually not a problem. As long as they're not urgent I can reschedule them for the next day.

I try to keep my goals in line with the moods I'm experiencing at the time. During times when I have a lot of energy my plans become ambitious. When I feel depressed I don't plan as much. I've found it wise to try to keep goals within reasonable reach, but not too easy either. Always stretching a little bit further and a little bit higher helps a person grow. Writing down what I want to accomplish can also help me see when I'm in danger of overdoing things.

These days, as I awake from my slumbers in my usual fog, I study my diary to see what I've set out for myself to do. My goals soon come into focus. I become enthused about the day. I sense the preciousness of the hours ahead. There is something to get up for!

Finding Meaning In Life

Lives based on having are less free
than lives based either on doing or being.
– William James

Finding meaning in life is learning to know what really matters to us. Most of us who have found something meaningful in life find our enthusiasm for each day to be strong. Understanding what matters gives us a sense of purpose and direction. We become eager about life and the abundant possibilities it holds for us.

Money is something we all obviously value because we need it to survive. We spend most of our lives working to earn sufficient supplies of it to buy us what we need. But many truly happy people have learned that there are values beyond the worth of having possessions alone. They learn there's more than just money to strive for: loving and being loved, appreciating the beauty of the world, enjoying music and other art forms. We can find value in the work we do – in doing our personal best at whatever we try.

Many of us find meaningful satisfaction by giving our talents in the form of volunteer work – especially if our nine-to-five job isn't sufficiently fulfilling. Once we have found where our personal set of values lies we have the choice to go in the direction that feels right for us. We learn to use our time and energy productively.

Doing our best to involve ourselves in meaningful work may find us participating in the work of the community. Personal interests may become less important and our focus may instead turn to how we can serve society. As we put increasingly more energy into the work we've committed ourselves to, no matter what it may be, our hopes will increase and we'll recognize the scope of possibilities that lie before us.

Volunteer opportunities are endless for those who are eager to work but unable to work under the stress of the paid workforce. They can work with children, seniors, physically and mentally challenged individuals, and many other groups of people. Why not read to or write letters for the blind, be a volunteer shopper for shut-ins, or visit those in hospital?

To find volunteer positions contact a local health department, volunteer agency, or your church. In this great big world there are many who could benefit from your help. Often this volunteer work can give enough experience to prepare you for a paying position.

Meaning in life is unique for each of us – very few people have the same set of values and goals. Only we ourselves can decide what is meaningful for us. When we have found it and know what our values are, other people's opinions cannot change who we are and what we stand for. We have affirmed ourself as an individual, with the courage of our own convictions.

When we have found what matters most in our life we will have strong protection against debilitating depression. It's easier to escape "down" moods when there is purpose in the day – when challenging activities await.

There may still be times of depression. But we will have the tools to fight it and make it less severe and less long-lasting.

Pursuing a Goal

The secret of success is constancy of purpose.
– Benjamin Disraeli, Speech, June 24,1872

What a great feeling! The car is packed, all last-minute preparations have been made, and we're finally ready to start rolling toward our destination.

As we begin traveling down the highway we feel free, full of purpose, in control. The traffic is fairly light today. Our optimism builds; we feel strong.

We enjoy the drive through the countryside, between grand mountains and past shimmering lakes. There are so many interesting things to see – so much we could explore! Only something serious can keep us from our goal. We are determined to go the distance it takes to reach it. We know that as long as we keep moving toward it we will feel that sense of control and our hopes will stay in focus.

And so it is with our lives. Once we have chosen a meaningful purpose (or destination) and we believe in it and start moving toward it, we *will* feel strong and in control.

Many people go through their entire lives aimlessly, not really working toward a specific goal. Some people think that everything that happens to them is somehow given to them by fate – whether it's a blessing or a curse. But, in fact, much of what we gain in life is a direct consequence of what we ourselves do to obtain it. It's up to us to choose the road that's right for us, and to travel it.

There *will* be frustrations – major ones and minor ones. All roads traveled have occasional tie-ups, or even accidents. Sometimes we get sick and have to rest and recover before continuing. But if our goal is important to us and we believe that our setbacks are only temporary (as most are), we *will* be able to keep our eyes focused on that destination. Soon we'll start traveling again and feel the joyous exhilaration that comes from moving toward something worthwhile.

Overcoming Obstacles

I have learned that success is to be measured
not so much by the position that one has reached in life
as by the obstacles which one has overcome while trying to succeed.
– Booker T. Washington, *Up from Slavery*

But what if a problem comes up (as it undoubtedly will): the road to our goal is blocked or we make a mistake and things don't work out as planned? What if we get sick?

Obstacles are common on any road. How we respond to them will determine how well we will succeed with our goals. We should remember that our mistakes and downfalls are not necessarily failures, but only other stages toward our goal, lessons we can learn from. The only *real* failure comes when we don't even try. A baby does not learn to walk on its first attempt. Neither should we expect to succeed without falling down once in a while. It's all part of the natural process.

Persistence helps us develop an optimistic attitude. Optimism, or having faith in our ability to succeed, will become increasingly stronger as we gain more accomplishments.

When our purpose is strong, we tend to ignore small frustrations. We feel energetic and don't notice minor aches and pains. We realize our time is valuable and we can focus on the work we want to do. When we approach our lives in this positive fashion, nothing can truly block our path; we will always find a way to continue. Bouts of illness are only temporary setbacks for most of us.

Alexander Graham Bell said, "When one door closes, another opens; but we often look so long and so regretfully upon the closed door that we do not see the one which has opened for us." Often what seems like an obstacle can actually be a blessing. An obstacle can force us to explore alternate routes to solve our problems – routes we might otherwise not have thought of. We need to be able to see that good can come out of bad; we may then find that we only have to change direction or adapt our methods.

Thomas Edison had worked for years to perfect the electric light bulb when he was asked if he wasn't discouraged by all his failures. "No," he said, "because I now know about 3000 things that do not work." This is the kind of attitude we need to be successful.

Work Is Precious

My share of the work of the world may be limited,
but the fact that it is work makes it precious...Green, the historian,
tells us that the world is moved not only by the mighty shoves of the heroes,
but also by the aggregate of the tiny pushes of each honest worker.
– Helen Keller

Many people living with mood disorders are able to have careers. But some of us are limited in what we can do. Even with medications our mood fluctuations can make it difficult to have a regular job.

But our limitations do not have to hold us back from becoming valuable members of our community. We *do* have periods when we are well. With a meaningful goal and determination, we can use these healthy times to accomplish things.

Helen Keller had a strong desire to communicate her ideas and, in spite of the limitations placed on her by both her deafness and blindness, she learned how. She left a legacy of writing that is an inspiration to all, especially to those with handicaps.

We, like Helen Keller, may be limited in how much we can do, but that doesn't mean we can't accomplish something worthwhile. What matters is not how *much* time and energy we are able to devote to our work, but how *well* we use the resources we have. The hours of our life flow into and out of the passing days at what seems like an ever-increasing speed. It would be a waste not to use them well to build a fruitful, satisfying life.

Every day becomes so precious and meaningful when we fill it with work we believe in and love. Whether it's working for the social good, building a small business, creating beautiful things, or cooking delicious meals. What stirs our enthusiasm is not important; what is important is that it's right for *us*. Whether we work at a paying job or a part-time volunteer position, as long as we're doing something worthwhile and feel that we are contributing, our work can be a rich source of joy.

On Climbing Mountains

I find it strange how people are so focused on the future, on achieving their goals. They seem to be perpetually reaching for something, but when they reach it, it's not enough – they always need more. Satisfaction eludes them.

If my life's work were like a mountain, the value would be in the climbing of its peaks. Reaching the top would be the goal, but the truest joy would be in the climbing. When I get to the top and have spent some time looking around, I soon begin to get bored again.

The work that I love to do, work that is important to me, is my most cherished asset. I feel rich when I'm asked to take on interesting projects. It is satisfying to be able to use my abilities to do something useful. It's a joy to know each day is full of worthwhile things to do.

Work Becomes a Possibility

Soon after my release from the psychiatric hospital, feeling that I needed to work if I was going to feel good about myself again, I asked for a job at an office where I had been employed the previous summer. I explained what had happened to me and offered to work for free until I became more rehabilitated. Although working full-time was difficult and I did eventually end up having to work only half-time, I was able to make a steady income for about seven years. My life was not easy but I had an understanding boss who, in spite of my problems, tended to give me challenging projects to work on. I was happy to have these challenges entrusted to me; they helped build my confidence.

In the meantime, I got married and a few years later had a son. My role became that of a mother at home. I spent much time on creative activities, such as needlework and cooking. Photography became a consuming hobby at which I learned to excel. I was often asked to judge and speak at camera clubs.

As my son grew and he needed me less, I began to yearn for more re-sponsibilities outside the home. I wanted the satisfaction of earning some of my family's income.

Since those days, I have tried my hand at many things and have learned much and gained confidence in the process. I have published notecards, cook-books, and inspirational booklets for seniors. I've done freelance photography for newspapers, magazines, health and educational organizations. (Freelancing is a great way for people with mood swings to earn money. It's possible to vary the amount of work we do, according to how we are feeling.)

My mood disorder makes the possibility of a normal nine-to-five job diffi-cult for me (although many people with the same problems have found they can cope). But my illness has also been an advantage in my working life. The creative tendencies I possess, possibly due to my disorder, have encouraged a positive, imaginative approach to all I do.

Building: Skills, Talents, Hobbies, Career

Small opportunities are often the beginning of great enterprises.
– Demosthenes (c.384–322 BC)

Any activities we undertake, even those that seem insignificant, can be-come the basis for a serious hobby or maybe even a career. If we find en-joyment in an activity, there is a possibility that it's something we could become really good at. On these skills and talents we can build our lives, find fulfillment, and perhaps even make money to support ourselves.

Good skills don't appear on their own. We may think we're not cut out to have them – but *everyone* has an inherent capability they can build on. If we allow ourselves to be aware of the sparks of interest within us, and then follow up by actively pursuing this interest, we may well have the germ of a new hobby or career. These skills can grow into something we will want to work hard at so we can excel. We may find that what started as a casual pastime eventually becomes a serious undertaking. We might decide to go to school, study in earnest, and develop a career.

Constantly developing our skills and talents is key. We should persist in exploring new possibilities so that our enthusiasm will stay alive and grow. We may learn to do things in a way that no one else has thought of, carving a little area of expertise for ourselves, a little niche that is uniquely ours.

Encouragement acts as an important catalyst to building our abilities. If we were among the lucky children whose parents encouraged them, we will have had a good start. For adults there are clubs, organizations, and workshops that can support us in our efforts. It's a good idea to try some of these, both to receive help and to learn how our work compares with that of others. A club or adult education class provides a great place to make friends with people who have an interest similar to ours.

Whatever activities interest us – whether it be a craft, an art, mechanical work, a sport, or a business endeavor – they can develop in us a sense of confidence and purpose when we work hard at them. These are important ingredients for a happy life and will give us good reason to look forward eagerly to each new day.

With the Help of a Camera Club I Learn

Eager to pursue our photography hobby, Wes and I joined a camera club a few months after we were married. It quickly became an important part of our lives. Before long we were caught up in the activities and operation of the club. Although members were of all ages and backgrounds, we felt very much at home within this friendly group. What's more, we quickly learned photography.

How we enjoyed this new hobby! We spent our Sundays exploring the countryside, photographing everything from spring wildflowers to old deserted barns.

Every Thursday night was club night. The club members became like family to us, sharing our joys. With them we discovered new and different ways to use our cameras. We competed in a friendly way, never ceasing to learn new things from each other, yet each finding a uniqueness in his (or her) own approach. In later years, Wes and I were to find markets for our photographs – another source of satisfaction.

At the camera club, I grew in maturity and gained confidence, gradually taking more active roles, even spending a year as president. My self-esteem was healthy. I had learned a skill. I felt good about myself.

Responsibility

One bird cannot fly to heaven with another bird's wings.
– Thomas Adams

To be a full member of our family and community, we have to be willing to take responsibility for ourselves and everything that's meaningful in our lives. We all need to have an active role in the work that has to be done. This is important, not just for the sake of our self-esteem, but also to give us some measure of control over our situation. If we do not accept personal responsibilities our lives will end up being controlled, not by ourselves but by others, and by circumstances and conditions outside ourselves.

Examples of responsibilities some of us have are doing our share of household duties, parenting, doing volunteer work, or earning income. Taking responsibilities could mean taking a role in contributing to the welfare of our community. When we can take our responsibilities seriously, we'll feel good about ourselves; we'll be contributing to the world we live in. What's more, we'll find that when someone or something depends on us, somehow we become stronger; we forget our own problems.

One of the most basic responsibilities we should try to live up to is the responsibility for our own health. There is a tendency to wait passively for our doctors and medications to cure us. This does not accomplish anything – we are then only persisting in playing the role of victim.

When fate has dealt us a blow, when we've become sick and suffer, the healthiest attitude is to learn how to deal with it and carry on. Our doctor can give us pills and encouragement, but *we* are in the best position to make ourselves *really* well.

It's when we carry our fair share of responsibilities that we will have the ability to gain independence. We'll be free from other people's care as much as possible, thereby being the most complete person we can be. We'll be free to have the kind of life we want to have.

Vows of a Wife and Mother

"My cup is overflowing! Oh God, help me!" I pleaded. I barely got this out as I talked to Dr. McDougall on the phone. He understood what I meant – and what effort it took to press these words from my exhausted being.

"Would you like me to get you a bed in hospital, Marja?" he asked, both of us knowing that we were now using our last resort.

I was four months pregnant and had, for the baby's sake, been living without my usual anti-psychotic medications for three months. I was now paying for this lack of chemical balancing.

A few days later, in hospital, and back on my regular medication, I vowed I would fulfill my role as wife and mother. These roles were my priority now. This was what I would live for – in spite of my severely psychotic state, in spite of the anemia that had been sapping my strength.

I knew I had good reasons to get well: a husband, a home, and soon, a baby. I would trust my doctor and the medications he prescribed and be an obedient patient.

Over and over I repeated my vows within my head: I must be a good wife. I must be a good mother. I must be a good wife. I must be... I must do everything in my power to live up to my responsibilities. I must get well. I must focus on what are my most important roles at this time. I must, I must, I must...

Soon I began walking around the grounds for exercise – fearfully at first. Then down the street. Finally along the entire sidewalk that went around the hospital complex. I became stronger every day, mentally and physically. My breathing came from deeper places in my lungs; the world around me became more real.

And each day I used my free time sitting on my bed, finishing half-done cross-stitch projects, overdue gifts for my sister and for a friend. I was determined not to waste my time while in hospital.

And finally, I baked cookies. What better gift for Wes when he came to visit! What better way to give him reason to have faith in me. With the help of an activity worker, I used the kitchen on the ward. With much fiddling and searching we found the ingredients for peanut butter cookies.

Slowly, in my confused and clumsy state, I worked – almost using detergent powder instead of sugar, cutting a finger on the edge of the peanut butter can.

Lunchtime came as I was baking. In between putting sheets of cookies into the oven and taking them out again, I ate a little and took sips of coffee. I felt almost normal again!

Coping With Big Responsibilities

I've always enjoyed the challenge of responsibilities. It's important to me to play a vital role in any organization I belong to, whether it's a club, the church, or my son's scouting troop. But, after years of manic depression, I learned to recognize that I could never count on being well. My frequent mood swings made me wary of my ability to carry out big responsibilities. I could never forecast when depression, mania, or psychosis would take over and make normal functioning impossible. And yet, I could not be happy without having a significant part in my community's activities.

Gradually, I found that it was possible to build a support system for my more important jobs or projects. I engaged assistants to work with me. They could then cover for me should I become sick.

Two big roles I accepted some years ago were as president of a large club and as publications chairperson for a major conference. In each case, I recruited someone to work closely with me, always keeping them informed of what I was doing and giving them a share of the work. I shouldered the major part of the job and made final decisions. I explained to my helpers that I had a health problem which sometimes cropped up and that they were important to me as a back-up. They seemed to respect how I handled the situation and realized that they served an important function.

During the planning of the conference, I did get sick. The assistant took over very capably for a few weeks. I was able to work on my recovery without a feeling of guilt, knowing that the work was in good hands. Soon I was able to take the reins again. It didn't matter that I didn't do it all by myself. Our part of the work for the conference turned out to be a great success. Although I needed to lean on someone else, I felt that I had guided the work and contributed in a major way.

I've found that, the older I get, the more I understand how my illness affects me. I've learned how much I can do and what I need to avoid doing. I often say "yes" to requests for help; and I often say "no" as well. I've learned to judge what I can safely handle on my own and where I have to get support. Having to ask for support is nothing to be ashamed of. Most people in responsible positions need assistants: executives of companies, professional people, even the president of the United States. Getting occasional support, especially for the bigger things I want to accomplish, makes it possible for me to play the kind of part I want to play in my community.

Stepping Stones of Life

He lifted me out of the slimy pit,
out of the mud and mire;
he set my feet on a rock
and gave me a firm place to stand.
He put a new song in my mouth...
– Psalm 40:2–3

Many people aren't aware that just because we have an affective disorder doesn't mean we're sick all the time. Most of us have long periods when we function normally. During these well times there's much we can accomplish.

Everyone has good times and bad times. Those of us with mood disorders have a bigger than average share of highs and lows. If we use our imagination, we can look at these fluctuations in our well-being as though they were smooth, flat stepping stones placed in a murky slough. The stepping stones represent our good times; the muddy spaces in between symbolize our low times.

When we are on the stepping stones, we are best able to be productive. We really must make the most of these times.

We should think of these stones as the level plateaus of wellness on which we can build our life: making friends, doing creative work, learning skills, achieving our best. We can use these times to find the places in the community where we feel at home and can contribute. When down times come, the support systems we'll have developed and the positive elements we've built into our lifestyle become protection that will help us.

If we use our well times to build energetically, we will find our down times to be mere spaces between the stepping stones of our life, something we try not to pay too much attention to. We focus on the life we build while we're on the solid platforms of the stones. Those muddy spaces don't really count, except that, each time we sink into them and climb back out again onto a new stepping stone, we find our enthusiasm for life is renewed.

Reminders

When I become psychotic and am not able to do what I normally would, my confidence starts lagging very quickly. But thankfully I have spent the time while I was well in a productive way and the good things in my life and my achievements help me to feel better.

Around me are reminders of things I've accomplished: the very special needlework picture I worked so hard on, the photographs I've made and the awards I received for them. I am grateful for my comfortable home and the husband and son who have loved me through my ups and downs. While I'm sick I'm not able to pursue the goals I believe so strongly in, but just knowing they're there, waiting for me to return to them again later, helps me feel more positive.

Memories of what I accomplished during the time I was functioning well reach out to me, slowly coming back to support and comfort me when I'm not well. Building my self-esteem while I was strong and capable has assured that I will have something to draw from at times when I need it.

Thank God for Today

I can't say that I'm happy about having a mental illness. At times I've suffered miserably. But what I've gone through has taught me so much – and for this I'm thankful.

Having lost months to psychosis and depression has helped me value highly the times when I'm well. Good health is so very precious – when I have it I try to make the most of it. I try as much as I can to use my energy and time to accomplish what I hope will be useful work.

I try to embrace each day as a precious gift and do what I can with it. I have dreams that I want to work toward and *Today* is the day I must use to try to do that. I don't like to wait for tomorrow. *Today* is the only day I can be sure I'll have. When tomorrow does come, I'll probably have other plans I'll want to bring to fruition.

Life can be exhilarating when I use it to actively accomplish things. Living my well times has become a delicious challenge with rewards at every turn. Somehow I feel that, without having experienced severe illness, I would not be appreciating what I have as much. I would not realize the treasure I have in living for *Today*.

9

THE CREATIVE RESPONSE

The Creative Response

Is getting well ever an art,
or art a way to get well?
– Robert Lowell, *Unwanted*

As we saw earlier, the "relaxation response" is a form of therapy designed to help people cope with stress. Each time you feel the effects of stress, you respond by inhaling deeply, holding your breath briefly, then letting the air out again as you relax fully. Once you recognize the stress symptoms, you automatically do the exercise.

I have found that, as the "relaxation response" can help stress, so a "creative response" can help to fight the onset of depression.

Being creative could be looked on as the direct opposite of being depressed. Creativity brings brightness, color, energy, and joy. Depression is characterized by darkness, lethargy and sadness. Creativity builds, while depression keeps us in a static state.

Living a creative lifestyle filled with interesting projects that make us feel alive will help ward off depression. When something like art or craft projects – or even creating new business plans or redecorating a home – engage us, we should be filled with sufficient enthusiasm so that "down" times become less frequent.

But, at those times when we *do* start to feel the subtle hints of an oncoming depression – when life starts to feel flat and pointless – that's the time to bring the "creative response" into play.

This is the time to begin work on something new and stimulating. It's the time to engage ourselves in something that will fill us with an eager sense of purpose. Embracing a creative activity will push us forward toward a new goal. With this fresh dose of ambition the depression that threatened may not take hold at all – and, if it does, it may be short-lived.

So each time we begin to feel that old dullness, we must try to brighten it with something we enjoy doing. Our projects can be big or small; it all depends on our own ambition or what we have the time or money for. We could plant a garden, write a poem or story, paint a picture, or plan an advertising campaign. It's vital that what we do fills the hunger we have to bring a rainbow into a world that often seems so gray.

Protection Against My Depression

Except for a period of creativity in childhood, I was not really creative until in my early 20s, after my first serious bout of illness. Then I learned to use creative activities as protection against the strong moods that so often threatened.

While I was recovering from several months at a psychiatric hospital and trying to learn how to live with my illness, I began to do needlework and photography. I wanted to make things that would outlast me. If I were to die, I wanted my life to have counted for something. Being sick had made me aware of the value of being well and I wanted to use the life I had in the best possible way. I looked on the time I had spent sick as wasted and was determined that the rest of my life would serve a useful function. Through arts and crafts, I was going to put something into the world instead of taking from it. Whether I was right or wrong – this is how my thinking went.

So I made photographs and needlepoint pictures and poured all my energy into these projects. It felt good to hold up a finished product and know that I had made it.

Doing creative work kept depression away – or at least made it less severe. Whenever I felt it coming on, I used to look for a colorful, exciting new project to work on. Focusing my energies on these things took my mind off the negative and helped remove the approaching shadow of depression.

Now, 25 years later, creativity still makes up a major part of my lifestyle. My life is filled with productive work that ranges from cooking a casserole to writing a magazine article to photographing the poppies in our garden. And I know that the benefits to my health are immeasurable.

Life Sparkles

To me, the highest form of living is when I'm engaged in a creative activity. In fact, life would be a downright bore if I didn't have the opportunity to make things. Being creative brings color and excitement to my days. It injects my life with joy and makes it precious.

Each time a new idea is born in my mind I become like a sculptor with a fresh block of clay. Eagerly I start shaping, my imagination freely coming into play. The delicious challenges that come with creating test my resourcefulness. It's fun to see how well I can carry out a project – to see if I can produce something good.

I love making beautiful pictures to communicate my feelings and try to arouse in others the sense of awe I feel about the world. In doing this I do the best I can, knowing that the more perfect the picture, the stronger my statement will be.

I need film for my camera like I need food for my stomach. The film allows me to satisfy my hunger for images. At times I have an almost insatiable appetite for these. The table is spread before me. I approach it eagerly.

I can truly say life sparkles when I'm making things happen. Working on creative projects makes me feel that I'm contributing something to the world that wasn't there before – something that only I can contribute in my own particular way. I feel productive. I gain a sense of vitality.

Artists with Mood Disorders

The fires of a supreme zest for living and the most gnawing desire
for death alternate in my heart, sometimes in the course of a single hour.
I know only one thing: I cannot go on like this!
– Gustav Mahler

There has long been a belief that genius and "insanity" are in some way related. History reveals countless examples of artists who suffered from both depression and manic depression. Writers such as Mark Twain, Lord Byron, William Blake and Edgar Allan Poe, and painters and composers such as Georgia O'Keeffe and Frederic Chopin were all affected.

It must be emphasized, though, that most people with mood disorders do not necessarily have greater talent, and most artists do not suffer from a mood disorder. But studies *have* shown that people with mood disorders (as well as their relatives) exhibit greater creativity than individuals who have no history of psychiatric disorders.

In the February 1995 issue of *Scientific American*, Dr. Kay Redfield Jamison, a leading clinician-scholar described her findings that, in her research of bipolar disorder amongst highly gifted artists, "Manic-depressive illness and creative accomplishment share certain noncognitive features: the ability to function well on only a few hours of sleep, the focus needed to work intensively, bold and restless attitudes, and an ability to experience a profound depth and variety of emotions."

According to DSM-IV (the Diagnostic and Statistical Manual of Mental Disorders) during mild mania (or hypomania) "the change in functioning for some individuals may take the form of a marked increase in efficiency, accomplishments, or creativity... The increase in goal-directed activity may involve planning of, and participation in, multiple activities. These activities are often creative and productive."

Creative people who are constantly tossed from highs to lows, from lethargy to high activity, from joy to sadness can turn their chaos and pain to good use in their artistic endeavors. They can recognize, in a more vivid way than most, the sharp contrasts of life and use this understanding to create inspired art.

Those Not Altogether Unlike Us

As sufferers of depressive disorders, we're by no means alone. We are in good company. In the epilogue to his book entitled *Moodswing*, Dr. Ronald Fieve (one of the first doctors to prescribe lithium) wrote, "...people who suffer from the illness in its milder forms of moodswing tend to be magnificent performers, magnetic personalities, and true achievers. Many superachievers in business, the arts, and especially in politics are hidden hypomanics (having a mild form of mania)."

Below is a list of famous people who are believed to have had unipolar or bipolar affective disorders. It is by no means complete.

Diane Arbus, Photographer	Robert Burns, Poet
Hans Christian Andersen, Author	Lord Byron, Poet
Honoré de Balzac, Author	Frederic Chopin, Composer
Brendan Behan, Author	Winston Churchill, Prime Minister
Irving Berlin, Composer	Kurt Cobain, Rock Star
William Blake, Author	Samuel Coleridge, Poet

Oliver Cromwell, Politician
Charles Darwin, Explorer
King David, Biblical Figure
Emily Dickinson, Poet
Fyodor Dostoevsky, Author
Patty Duke, Actress
Thomas Eagleton, U.S. Senator
Thomas Edison, Inventor
Edward Elgar, Composer
Queen Elizabeth I, Monarch
Ralph Waldo Emerson, Author
F. Scott Fitzgerald, Author
Sigmund Freud, Psychiatrist
Paul Gauguin, Painter
Johann Goethe, Author
Francisco de Goya, Painter
Georg Fredrich Handel, Composer
Nathaniel Hawthorne, Author
Ernest Hemingway, Author
Howard Hughes, Industrialist
Victor Hugo, Author
Heinrich Ibsen, Playwright & Poet
Job, Biblical Figure
Joan of Arc, Religious Leader
Robert E. Lee, General
Abraham Lincoln, President
Martin Luther, Religious Leader
Gustav Mahler, Composer

John Milton, Poet
Benito Mussolini, Dictator
Sir Isaac Newton, Physicist
Florence Nightingale, Nurse
Georgia O'Keeffe, Painter
Boris Pasternak, Author
Sylvia Plath, Author
Edgar Allen Poe, Author
Ezra Pound, Author
Cole Porter, Composer
Sergei Rachmaninoff, Composer
Theodore Roosevelt, President
Robert Schumann, Composer
Percy Bysshe Shelley, Poet
Emanuel Swedenborg, Religious
    Leader
P. I. Tchaikovsky, Composer
Alfred Lord Tennyson, Poet
Dylan Thomas, Author
Leo Tolstoy, Author
Mark Twain, Author
Vincent van Gogh, Painter
Queen Victoria, Monarch
George Washington, President
Walt Whitman, Poet
Tennessee Williams, Playwright
Virginia Woolf, Author

These are men and women who learned to rise above their unipolar and bipolar mood disorders. They were fortunate to be able to make their moods work *for* them instead of against them. Through their suffering they understood more about life than those for whom life was easier.

Artists, politicians, and religious leaders like these can inspire us. Although most of us will not reach the high pinnacles of achievement these people did, they show us that our illness does not *have* to keep us from developing our own creative potential.

Our Passions, High and Low

The happiness of a man in this life does not consist in the absence but in the mastery of his passions.
– Alfred Lord Tennyson

The passionate moods that result from our illness and cause us so much suffering can actually be beneficial if we use what we learn from them to express ourselves creatively. Throughout history artists have used the feelings they have as a source of inspiration for their work. The feelings we experience are extreme: the depths of depression for those with a unipolar disorder and the alternating lows and highs for those with a bipolar disorder.

The frequent presence of these moods makes us a very sensitive group of people. When depressed we sense the depths of the world's sorrows more keenly – feelings most people filter out. Although the sun is shining, the world seems dark and without meaning. Those of us who experience highs know what it is to be transported to what seems like heavenly flights of joy – even if the source of this joy may be as simple as poppies blowing in the wind. We cry in mourning for the realities of injustice, poverty, and sickness we see around us; and we dance to celebrate the truths of love and beauty.

The strong emotions we experience make life more difficult; but they can also make life richer for us. In a way it is good to feel strongly; sensitivity is an aspect of humanity that sets us apart from much of the animal kingdom. Our expansive capacity for passion gives us the inspiration which makes artists out of many of us. We have a need to express and share our feelings with others. Creative activity is our way of venting the contents of our hearts; there's too much to keep shut up inside. By mastering the techniques of our chosen medium, we learn to apply the discipline needed to harness our emotions and to steer them into workable pieces of art. The result is an abundance of satisfaction and sense of fulfillment for the artist – and often a healing of the soul.

But what about those of us who don't feel we are creative? *There may be more of the artist in us than we think.* We can let go of our emotions through song and dance, through laughter and the healing of tears, and even through simply talking with others about our feelings. To reveal to others how we experience life is to share the rich tapestry of our inner self in all its colors. This kind of sharing by others, not unlike us, has left us a great legacy of paintings, sculpture, music, and literature. If we can use our passions effectively they will be a rich source of joy, not just for us, but also for those around us.

Art as Medicine

When I was young, I remember being sick and staying home from school. I would spend my day in bed, usually one made up for me in the living room. My mother worked around me, dusting and vacuuming. I felt protected and comforted in the bed – far from the stresses of school. There were no demands on me from anywhere; my time was my own.

At times like this I was the most creative. Although I was sometimes sick with fever and weakness, as I began to recover I was able to summon the energy to work on something like knitting a stuffed animal for a young nephew.

It's been said that art (or any creative work, for that matter) has an ability to heal. It seemed to work wonders for me when I was young. In spite of being physically sick, I could comfort myself by making things. The satisfaction I felt when I saw the completed project was worth the effort it took to make.

Since that time I've used the healing power of being creative in my sick times with manic depression in the same way. When it's difficult to fulfill normal responsibilities, I can help myself feel better by doing small creative projects. I don't feel up to everything at times like this – and it is very hard to focus – but by trying hard there are simple things I can do to help me feel some sense of accomplishment. And I do feel that I get better sooner as a result.

Our Need to Be Unique

Every individual has a place to fill in the world, and is important
in some respect, whether he chooses to be so or not.
– Nathaniel Hawthorne

It is important for each of us to feel unique. We find life more meaningful if we can make a contribution that is solely ours to give. Being creative makes us feel very much like an individual. No other person in the world possesses our precise combination of ideas, talents, and abilities. We can make things and do things (not necessarily art alone) that could never be done in the same particular way by any other person.

Ask a group of photographers to capture a sunrise, and no two will do it in the same way. There are so many variables, in angles, lenses, film, and composition to choose from. Each of us is an individual who will choose our own way of doing things.

Freeing up our spirits and honestly expressing ourselves through our handiwork is liberating. Life becomes more joyous – more purposeful. We set our frustrations loose and instead, create something meaningful of our very own.

The events and feelings we experience differ from those experienced by others. These will contribute to how we express ourselves and when we declare our uniqueness, our confidence in ourselves as an individual will grow.

Child's Play

Know you what it is to be a child?...
It is to be so little that the elves can whisper in your ear;
it is to turn pumpkins into coaches, and mice into horses,
lowness into loftiness, and nothing into everything...
– Percy Bysshe Shelley

Do you remember how much fun it was when you were a child – playing with clay, crayons, paints, and colorful paper? We played without any grand sense of purpose, content to explore and create for the pure joy of it. We had a sense of freedom in those precious years. It was natural to give expression to our feelings and to our sense of wonder. Our art materials made it possible to create almost anything our imagination summoned forth. How content we were to dabble!

Have you ever thought of taking the time, one rainy afternoon, to invest in some wonderful, brightly colored felts or other art materials, and to turn once more to an hour or two of happy play? We could shut the world's problems off, turn on our favorite music, and apply beautiful greens, yellows, and reds to paper. We wouldn't worry about how good it looks or whether it's sophisticated enough. We could take time to be kids again for just a little while, solely for the joy of it! We could let go and allow our feelings to have free rein. Play – marvelous, relaxing, easy play – too marvelous to reserve for little children alone.

Creative activity like this can reduce the stresses of our busy lives. It will allow us to feed our emotional energy into something that is fun and positive. Relaxed play frees us up and helps us to get in touch with our inner feelings – to reach into our heart and find the child we still have within.

In a Field of Buttercups

Seek not afar for beauty. Lo! it glows
In dew-wet grasses all about thy feet;
– Minot Judson Savage, *Earth's Common Things*

I lie in the midst of the buttercups, trying to capture the beauty of what seems, at a glance, to be so commonplace. The little flowers with their shiny faces seem to dance in carefree innocence. There's something I love about their simplicity and joy – something I can relate to. With my camera's macro lens I zoom in and out on the tiny golden blooms, on the grasses that are their neighbors, on the ladybug crawling up a narrow blade.

Lost in this natural world, I leave behind all my worries – all the complexities of life – and focus completely on the simple wonders of the everyday. This is one of my favorite ways to worship, to "smell the flowers," as they say.

This meadow is where I become a child again, kneeling and crawling close to the ground – seeing things from a humble angle. This is where I play, carefree and lost in the purest form of living I know. This is where I truly find myself, communing with God's wondrous creation.

To Be a Master

If people knew how hard I have had to work to gain my mastery,
it wouldn't seem wonderful at all.
– Michelangelo (1475–1564)

We tend to look at artists' work as something magically produced by individuals who were endowed with a God-given talent, a gift which allowed them to create with ease. As Michelangelo expressed in the quote above, producing wonderful art is not an easy job at all. The artist, however talented, has to work hard to produce great masterpieces.

This is how it is with any work of value that we attempt to produce – whether it's creating a sculpture, building a cabinet, knitting a sweater, or growing a colorful spring garden: each requires loving and patient dedication and much hard work.

A talent cannot be developed without love for the work. When we love a creative activity we don't mind devoting countless hours to make a masterpiece. This love can also inspire us to feed our strongest emotions into the piece, making it unique. We dip down into the bottomless reserve of resources we all have and express the sights, sounds, and feelings we experience. Love will give us the desire to strive for perfection.

Many of us have talents we're not even aware of. Some say that every one of us is born to be creative. But in some of us, creativity is encouraged while in others it's squelched. Could it be possible that we have talents we've never encouraged to grow – talents that, if we worked to develop them, could make it possible for us to do things we'd never dreamed of, or dreamed of but never dared to make reality?

When Our Imagination Takes Control

My thoughts bustle along like a Surinam toad,
with little toads sprouting out of back, side,
and belly, vegetating while it crawls.
– Samuel Taylor Coleridge, W. Jackson Bate's *Coleridge*

For those of us with manic depression, problems can develop when we get too carried away with activities that involve our imagination. Sometimes we become so totally consumed by the creative process, by the power we feel in what we're producing, that everything else in life becomes secondary. We often forget to eat or sleep. We put responsibilities on hold.

At times like this, our heads become so filled with our work that we tend to lose touch with the rest of the world. The project we're working on takes over. It becomes difficult to remember to look after the nuts and bolts of everyday life: to our needs and obligations. We feed our manic tendencies and get sick.

Mood-stabilizing medications can help many of us overcome this inclination to overrespond to our artistic spirit. But, in addition, it is still wise to be very careful to discipline ourselves, to work for shorter periods of time and to alternate creative work with more physical jobs like housework or gardening. It's not healthy to allow any single activity, however interesting or important, to take control of our life. It's important always to keep a balance, remembering the old adage to "do everything in moderation."

Begin It!

Whatever you can do, or dream you can, begin it.
Boldness has genius, power and magic in it.
– Johann Wolfgang von Goethe

You may not believe that you're talented. You may believe that talent is inherent in only a few people. Although it's true that there is a genetic factor, all of us *do* have innate abilities of one sort or another; they only need to be awakened.

Fear holds many of us back from trying creative activities. We're afraid that we won't succeed – that we'll be failures. As a result we don't try at all, and that truly *is* a failure.

We all have the ability to be a virtuoso in one field or another. To bring this ability out we must believe in ourselves. Special inborn gifts are not as significant as using whatever resources we *do* have to advantage. If we can learn to use whatever we have instead of complaining about what we lack, we will succeed.

I can't draw, but I can do photography. My sister, a dancer who was forced to retire, has found expression in sculpture, another three-dimensional art form. Someone uninterested in creating pieces of art may be very creative in how he or she gives support to a sick neighbor. Creativity is valuable in all fields of human endeavor.

Developing our own special area of creativity means, to begin with, being alert to what moves us. We must learn to listen to our heart when we see and hear the music and artwork around us. What excites us? What makes us feel good? Are we itching to try that technique ourselves? Do we feel inspired? As we move around our community looking at books, pictures, movies, theater, we may find something awaken inside us – a desire to try something ourselves.

When we become aware of this "tugging at the heart," it's important not to procrastinate, but to act on it. Procrastinating will only kill that delicious urge – that appetite – to make something of our own. It will postpone our opportunity to be empowered to speak, to have our unique voice heard through our creative projects. Today is the best day to begin finding the joy, satisfaction, and self-esteem that creativity can bring.

Conclusion

I'm not a teacher: only a fellow-traveller of whom you asked the
way. I pointed ahead – ahead of myself as well as you.
    – George Bernard Shaw, *Getting Married*

Although life has much joy and beauty, we know it has its challenges as
well. For those of us with mood disorders, this is especially so. There are
times when, even with relatively successful medications, we fall back into a
depression or gradually return to a state of mania. Our lives will probably
continue to be a bit like a roller-coaster ride. We have to prepare ourselves
for the ups and downs.

But there is much hope. It is encouraging to see the ongoing changes
in the field of psychiatry. Medications are steadily improving; and many
have fewer side effects as well. There is more reason than ever before to
believe in the possibility of wellness; there is more reason to persevere with
the treatment plan our doctors prescribe for us.

Every day, more of us are speaking out freely about our illness, gradually reducing the stigma attached to mental illnesses. Bringing the topic
into the open raises awareness and improves public understanding. This
understanding will surely encourage our community to focus more on the
needs of the mentally ill. It is my hope that this will result in more funds
becoming available for much-needed research, care, and housing.

Since my first episode of illness in 1965, I've learned so much. I feel
confident that with my doctor's care; a healthy, creative lifestyle; and faith
in a loving God; I never need to be as sick as I was then. Although I know
everyone's experience of life and illness is unique, I do hope that what I've
learned and passed on in this book will help you cope better as well.

Life is so full of possibilities. What we need is the courage and imagination to pursue goals, whether they be small or large. It *is* possible to rise
above our illness and create a life filled with the riches of peace, love, and
happiness.

We are much more than people with mental disorders alone; our lives
can have many facets. We can be a loving friend to others, and receive love
in return. We can find meaningful ways of contributing to our family's

and community's welfare. If we do this, we'll be in a position to offer a compassionate shoulder to others, some of whom may have helped *us* in the past. We'll feel good about ourselves, and justly so.

Appendix

National Headquarters for U.S. and Canadian Mood Disorder Self-Help Groups:

The Depression and Manic-Depression Association Of Canada
4 - 1000 Notre Dame Avenue
Winnipeg, Manitoba R3E 0N3
Tel. (204) 786-0987
Fax (204) 786-1906

National Depressive and Manic-Depressive Association (NDMDA)
730 N. Franklin, Ste.501
Chicago, IL 60610-3526
Tel. 1-800-826-3632
Fax (312) 642-7243
Website: www.ndmda.org

For information about mental illnesses and support for clients contact one of the following or one of their regional divisions or chapters:

Canadian Mental Health Association (National Office) (CMHA)
2160 Yonge Street, 3rd floor
Toronto, ON M4S 2Z3
Tel. (416)484-7750
Fax (416)484-4617
Website: www.cmha.ca

National Association for Mental Illness (NAMI)
200 N. Glebe Road, Ste. 1015
Arlington, VA 22203-3754
Tel. (703) 524-7600
Fax (703) 524-9094
Website: www.nami.org

National Mental Health Association
1021 Prince Street
Alexandria, VA 22314-2971
Tel. (703) 684-7722
Fax (703) 684-5968
Website: www.nmha.org

Internet Websites

- Internet Depression Resources List: provides a list of links to websites and gives brief descriptions of them.

  www.execpc.com/~corbeau/

- WWW Mental Health Server: A wonderful resource for all issues and information related to mental health. See also INTERNET LINKS at this site; there are hundreds.

  www.mentalhealth.com/

News Groups

alt.support.depression
soc.support.depression